WHEN BEAVER WAS VERY GREAT

STORIES TO LIVE BY

Sharon Steele

WHEN BEAVER
WAS VERY GREAT

STORIES TO LIVE BY

by Anne M. Dunn

with illustrations by Sharon L. White

Midwest Traditions, Inc.
Mount Horeb, Wisconsin
1995

Midwest Traditions, Inc. is a nonprofit educational organization devoted to the study and preservation of the folk history and traditional cultures of the American Midwest. Our publications serve to bring this rich, diverse heritage to broader public attention.

For a catalog of books and other materials, write:

Midwest Traditions
PO Box 320
Mount Horeb, Wisconsin 53572 USA
(telephone 1-800-736-9189)

ISBN 1-883953-07-3 (softcover)
ISBN 1-883953-08-1 (hardcover)
Library of Congress Catalog Card #95-75453

Manufactured in the United States of America
Printed on acid-free recycled paper

Editor: Philip Martin
Book Design: Lisa Teach-Swaziek, PeachTree Design

Publisher's Cataloging in Publication

    Dunn, Anne M.
        When Beaver was very great : stories to live by / by Anne M.
    Dunn ; with illustrations by Sharon L. White.
        p. cm.
        ISBN: 1-883953-07-3 (softcover)
        ISBN: 1-883953-08-1 (hardcover)

    1. Ojibwa Indians. 2. Ojibwa Indians – Tales.
    3. Folk literature, Indian. I. White, Sharon L., ill. II. Title.

    E99.C6D86 1995   970.004'973
                                              QBI95-20050

First Edition
10 9 8 7 6 5 4 3 2 1

Dedicated to
my grandmother,
who presented me with wings,
my mother,
who gifted me with strength,
my father,
who provided the wind,
and
my children,
who loaned me the sky.

CONTENTS

Preface   10

SPRING

How the People Came   17
The Storytellers   20
Our Foolish Friend   22
Tardiness and Webster   24
Sugar Bush   26
Spring Comes to Oak Point   32
When Earth Was New   34
The Thrush   37
The Little Beings   40
Rabbit and Otter   43
The River   46
Fisher's Reward   50
Firefly Watch   55
From the Fourth Hill   56
Charlie's Beans   57
The Promise   62
Uncle's Camera   64
Mothers of Brothers   66
Same-Same   67
The Children's Fire   68
Song of Reconciliation   70

SUMMER

Muskrat's Tail   75
Fire   78
When Beaver Was Very Great   80
The Stone Carver   84
Song of the Wild Horse   86
The Trophy   90
Pamela   92
Truckin' with Dad   93
The Skirt   95
Star Quilt   97
Shattered Trust   99
Distress   102
Never Alone Again   103
Daisy Blessings   107
Casket Practice Thwarted   109
Sir Walter of the Moonlight   111
Corn Dance   115
The First Bluebird   116
Mother Mountain   118

FALL

How Turtle Cracked His Shell	123
The Gift of Mahnomen	126
Shee-sheeb Brings a Message	127
Flagging the Lake	129
The Cornhusk Doll	131
The Buffalo Woman	133
Journey to the White Buffalo Calf	138
Peace Float	143
Leaving the Woods	144
Mom	146
Hunter's Rest	147
He Wanted to Die	149
Lost Child	151
The Rag Man	154
To Sweep a Floor	156
September Moon Walk	159
Fog Woman	162
Buffalo Wife	167
How Aspen Came	173
Butterflies	175
One Place to Turn	178
Blueberry Joy	182

WINTER

The Perfect Gift	187
The Song of the Flute	191
Oak Point Journal	194
New Snow	199
The Legend of the Red Oak	201
A Christmas Carol	203
Tamarack and Chickadee	205
Moon Daughter	207
The Coin	210
A Good Name for Bad Boy	214
When Santa Came to Visit	217
Franklin Avenue Christmas	218
Winter Walk	221

PREFACE

When I first read this collection of writings, I could not help but think of a book by another Anne: Anne Morrow Lindbergh. Set on a small, isolated island off Florida's Gulf Coast, Lindbergh's simple but profound book, *Gift from the Sea*, looks at three shells found on the beach and, through them, at life.

Anne Dunn's writings are set in another part of North America: the woodlands of the Upper Midwest. A member of the Ojibwe nation, Anne (born 1940) grew up in northern Minnesota. As a young girl, she received many gifts from the wonderful storehouse of oral legends and animal fables of the Ojibwe, especially from her mother, Maefred Vanoss Arey, and her grandmother, Frances Vanoss. Like many Native American children, Anne experienced life on reservation land (Leech Lake, White Earth, and Red Lake Reservations) and also lived for a time as a child in the nearest big city, Minneapolis. Eventually she became a licensed practical nurse, a mother of six, a newspaper reporter, and a professional storyteller. A writer since childhood, she began publishing her own newsletter, *The Beaver Tail Times*, in 1987.

In *When Beaver Was Very Great*, Anne Dunn's stories are gathered together for the first time. Her graceful writings reflect an approach that Lindbergh would understand: looking at human life through the windows of the natural world. Important lessons come from the elements of the northern woodlands — the plants and trees of the forests, the waters of lakes and rivers, the polished red agates of the Lake Superior region.

Other teachings come from representatives of "other nations" — Rabbit, Wolf, Bear, Turtle, Chickadee, and their comrades large and small. These animals still speak to humans (at least to those who listen) through the traditional tales of the Ojibwe and other tribes native to North America.

Anne Dunn also spins new tales — stories originally made for her children or for others in school classrooms, prison cells, battered women's shelters, peace rallies, university lecture halls, Native American gatherings. We are also introduced to members of Anne's family and to her own childhood memories, all woven into this tapestry of tales.

Individually, these stories tend to be small and quiet — like Beaver and most of his friends. Gathered together, however, the writings begin to unveil a greater, invisible order of things: the ways of the world on Turtle Island, an interlocked community of animal, plant, and human nations. The stories gently introduce values for a more considerate walk of life.

Most of the traditional stories are Ojibwe tales, originally found only in oral form. A few tales come from other nations, such as the Lakota and Mandan. However, even stories active in Ojibwe tradition may be originally from other sources. Good stories travel well and can drift into a tradition, and if they fit, easily take root.

Historically, the woodland Ojibwe (also spelled Ojibway) of the northern Great Lakes region were once commonly known to whites as the Chippewa (probably a corruption of the word Ojibwe). In their own language, they are *Anishinabe*, the first people.

Their traditional tales have been shaped, polished, and retold for many years — over Anne's life, her mother's, her grandmother's, and by prior generations of master Ojibwe storytellers. This rich, thoughtful way of remembering and listening to the voices of the world around us through stories has evolved over hundreds of years.

An outstanding description of the role of such storytelling was recounted by acclaimed nature writer Barry Lopez in a 1994 speech to a literary audience, the Upper Midwest Booksellers Association. He said, "In Alaska once, in a small village in the interior, I asked a man about storytelling and he said, 'As long as the stories that you tell help, then you're the storyteller. When the stories that you tell don't help anymore, then you're not the storyteller, even if you say you are.' "

Lopez also related a remarkable word used by the Inuit people of the eastern Arctic to describe a storyteller, *isumataq*, which can be translated, "the person who creates the atmosphere in which wisdom reveals itself."

Those in touch with traditions — native peoples and others — understand that helpful tales are not used to look at the past. They address the present. This weaving of old ways into new situations, customary into contempory life, reveals a path to wisdom found long ago by traditional peoples. Faced with difficult questions, they look for answers in the right places. Wisdom is found in good stories... with messages and messengers from the past, offering maps and friendly hands to guide us into the future.

In these writings, Anne extends her hand and leads us to new places, to old places. Shining with vision, these places are blessed with the richness of smallness — the gleam of an agate, the track of a field-mouse, the watery trail of a beaver swimming by.

Stories are small gifts. Brother Beaver and the other friends found in Anne's stories know a secret that they want to share. Good stories are the best gifts.

Philip Martin
Midwest Traditions

SPRING

SPRING

HOW THE PEOPLE CAME _____

IT WAS GRANDMOTHER of the Sea who brought mankind in a sack from beneath the waves. She presented it to Young Wolf who waited on the sandy shore.

"Carry this sack across the land. But do not open it until you reach the Great Lakes. I cannot tell you how terrible things will be if you open the sack prematurely." With this warning to Young Wolf, she slipped under the waves and departed.

Young Wolf carried the sack until he became tired, then he stopped to rest. As he sat near the sack, he became increasingly curious about its contents.

Finally he glanced about to see if anyone was watching... and quickly opened the sack. He was horrified to see several people tumble out and run away.

As Young Wolf struggled to retie the sack, Old Wolf came along and helped him. Old Wolf knew what had happened, but he said nothing.

Suddenly Young Wolf, being filled with shame, went off to hide in the woods and mourn.

Wolves still gather in the woods and moonlit hills, howling from their hiding places... reminding us of Young Wolf's remorse at having failed to deliver all the people to the good land.

So it was Old Wolf who took the sack and continued across the country. When he reached the Great Lakes, he carefully opened the heavy sack and released the people.

The people stepped out of the sack and looked at the land. They saw many animals, beautiful birds, and bright flowers. Birch trees stood all around and berries grew on low bushes. The water was full of fish and red agates gleamed in the sun. The people were happy and they thanked Old Wolf for bringing them to the good land.

Old Wolf left the people and went into the woods, where they heard him howling in joy because he had delivered so many people to the good land and the good life.

The people that accidentally escaped when Young Wolf opened the sack lived a very poor kind of life and were eventually forgotten.

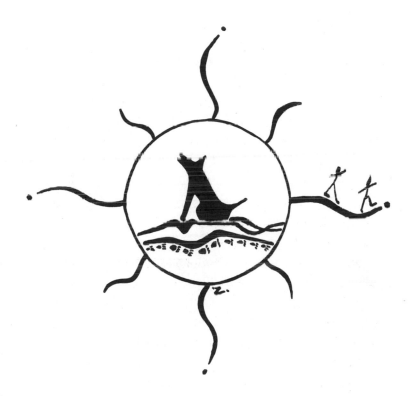

THE STORYTELLERS

L ONG AGO the Ojibwe had no written language. The "books" of the *Anishinabe* (Ojibwe for "the first people") were kept by the storytellers.

Some of the chapters were kept by those who remembered the history of the people: their travels and their wars.

Some of the chapters were kept by those who remembered the culture of the people: their myths and their legends.

Some of the chapters were kept by those who remembered the traditions of the people: their religion and their values.

I've been blessed with a family that loves to hear and tell good stories. It began with my grandmother Frances Vanoss. She was a keeper of fine tales. She told stories of adventure and traditional Ojibwe values.

Both my parents were storytellers, too. My father, Guy LaDuke, usually told funny stories. My mother, Maefred Arey, likes stories about animals.

So my days have been enriched by three wonderful storytellers, and having heard their tales again and again, I find that I have become a keeper of stories.

But those who keep stories must tell stories. If the stories are not told, they will be forgotten and lost... remembered only on paper pages or hoarded by historians and anthropologists.

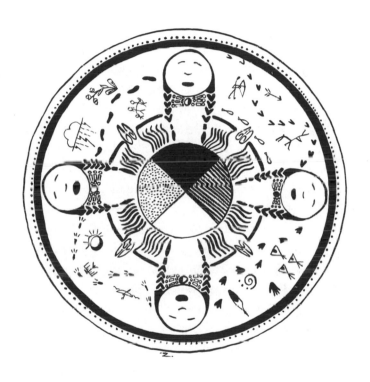

OUR FOOLISH FRIEND _____

O NE FINE EVENING in the long, long ago, our friend Rabbit came out of his snug burrow and found that a gentle snow was falling. He brushed bits of leaves and twigs from his big bushy tail and, being in good spirits, began to run in a large circle. Around and around he ran. As he ran... he sang a song.

As he ran... and as he sang... more and more snow fell. Soon, he noticed that the trees were getting shorter and shorter! He foolishly believed that his song caused this to happen, so he ran on... singing as he went.

At last he became very tired. Being unable to find his burrow, he settled down in the crotch of a little willow and went to sleep. He slept for two days!

As he slept, the weather became quite warm and the snow melted. The snow and frost spirits had suddenly returned to the far, far north. Spring had come to Rabbit's home in the swamp.

When Rabbit awakened, he found himself sitting high up in the crotch of a tall tree. Now, our friend Rabbit had never climbed a tree... and he'd never been very brave, either. So you can imagine how surprised and frightened he was to see what had happened.

Rabbit knew that he would certainly starve if he did not get out of the willow. He decided he would have to jump.

Well, he gathered all his courage... and it wasn't

much... closed his eyes and leaped. Just then... his nice, big bushy tail got caught in the crotch of the willow tree and broke off!

The force of his jump pushed his front feet back into his body, so they were now shorter than his hind legs. He also struck his face on a sharp stone and split his lip!

Now, every spring, the willows sprout little tufts of white fur to remind us that spring has come again... and to warn us not to be foolish like our poor little friend, Rabbit.

TARDINESS AND WEBSTER _____

THANKS to the Great Northern Railroad... tardiness was a regularly occurring phenomena during my secondary school years. But I must defend tardiness as, in my case, it prevented me from being ignorant.

We lived several blocks from school and there was no school bus service. Between our house and the school house lay the Great Northern Railroad tracks. It was busy in those days with much coming and going of many unhurried boxcars.

Morning often found me on the wrong side of the tracks, waiting for the early trains to pass. On such mornings, I knew the tardy bell would ring long before I crept into my desk.

But our principal at that time was a fairly reasonable and patient man. So of course he did not punish me for my first infraction. However, as my record increased, it became apparent that action must be taken to enhance my concept of punctuality.

Mr. Wood was a man of many books but his perennial favorite was Webster's Dictionary. Being the true educator which undoubtably he was, he brought Webster's great literary achievement to my myopic attention in a most resourceful manner.

Special after-school classes were arranged and I, with several other tardy-prone students, was invited to attend. Actually, he insisted upon it.

We were each presented with a much-abused, rarely-used edition of Webster's famous book and set to work copying copiously. We read and wrote feverishly for one stunning hour. It seemed as though I'd hardly begun when I was directed to desist.

After peering briefly at my hurried scrawl, Mr. Wood carefully tore the pages into several small contemptible pieces and deposited them unceremoniously into his wastebasket.

On my next visit to the class, I began using a notebook. When I explained that I wanted to save the pages and study them later, Mr. Wood seemed greatly shocked but extremely pleased. He initialed every page and returned the notebook. You can imagine how many notebooks I eventually filled.

So... now you can see why I must defend tardiness and thank the Great Northern Railroad for saving me from ignorance.

SUGAR BUSH

I REMEMBER the crusty snow crunching under our boots as we broke trail into the sugar bush. I remember that the cooking scaffold looked like a lonely skeleton with its arms flung out in welcome.

Like a grid, the scaffold shadow marked the place where we would build the fire. Digging down through the snow and matted leaves, we prepared a fireplace on the rich, dark forest soil. The children had already gathered bundles of dry sticks which they wigwammed over bits of paper and birchbark. The wigwam was lit on the wind-blown side and fed with larger sticks until a brisk blaze was leaping toward the sky.

Because we had no buildings there, at the end of the past sugaring season we had stacked our inverted catch-cans and cooking pails near the scaffold and covered them with tar paper held in place with heavy poles. Each year when we arrived, we dug them out, filled the pails with fresh snow, and hung them from the scaffold with strong wires. The fire licked eagerly at the black pails as we added more snow, until we had enough hot water to wash and rinse 300 catch-cans.

I have an especially vivid memory of the felling of a large dead maple. To our dismay we discovered it had been home to several flying squirrels. We quickly counted them as they glided down among the trees to seek new hiding places. It's quite unusual to see them during the day, and seven is more than most people will see in a lifetime.

As the men cut and split the wood, the women and children hauled it to camp on a long toboggan. There, they log-cabin stacked it like a fortress wall around the scaffold. The wall of wood would serve as a windbreak near the fire, where the logs would dry quickly if it should rain or snow. It took several days to get the wood ready. We knew there would be little time for gathering wood when the sap began to run.

When we had stacked enough wood... we went home to wait.

I watched the box elders near our home because we know that when the box-elders begin to weep... It's time to tap the maples.

In late winter, the sap rises up into the trees to begin another season of growth. The process is triggered by the fluctuating temperatures of cold, freezing nights followed by warm, thawing days.

How anxious we became as the days passed. At last we saw bright tears glistening in the branches of the box-elders. The sap was running!

We returned to camp with a brace-and-bit and a box of clean taps. The children distributed catch-cans. Small trees were tapped once on the sunrise side, so they would begin to flow early in the day. Larger trees would produce more sap and could be tapped more than once. One great tree held five cans well-spaced around its huge trunk. We called the tree "Grandfather."

We stood together to witness the tapping of the first tree. As the bit was turned, a long curl of moist wood was drawn out. When the bit was removed, a spout was placed in the hole and a can was quickly hung in place. We watched a drop of sap appear, glitter in the sunlight, fall from the spout, and splash into the bottom of the can with a musical "ting." With that drop... another harvest had begun!

Because the sweet-tasting sap is only about three-percent sugar, it may take more than thirty gallons of sap to produce one gallon of syrup. Boiling the sap to make syrup is long, hard work.

But although the sugar bush is a place of intense work, it is also a place of spiritual renewal and personal enrichment. It's hard to imagine a better place to be in March.

If I got to camp early, I'd find the sap still frozen in the spouts. I'd lay wood for a large fire, about eight feet long and three feet wide, fill the cooking pails with sap from the storage barrels, and hang the pails over the fire. Then I'd brew a pot of sap-coffee.

As the sun climbed into the sky, the grove began to warm, and I'd walk away from the snapping fire to listen to the sap song. I'd hear it begin far away. "Ting." The sap was thawed. "Ting." It fell into waiting catch-cans. "Ting. Ting." Soon I was surrounded by the happy rhythm. But as the cans began to fill, the song subsided... for only empty cans sing.

When I was young I used to think, "If we did not

come to release the maple sap, life would not return to the land. For life flows from this grove into all the world." Now, I think it strange to imagine we might deny spring by refusing to tap the maples. But nevertheless, I find it difficult to laugh at the wisdom of such foolishness.

Although the sugar bush enriched my life with quiet memories, it would never be complete without the laughter of happy children.

The children spent many hours swinging in the arms of an ancient maple broken by storms and years. The giant seemed unwilling to resign itself to the earth and, propped up on huge limbs, it invited the children to many adventures. They called it "the love tree," because they loved to play there.

The children also learned to be comfortable with wild things. Near the camp, two osprey made their summer home. Their ragged-looking nest clung to the top of a dead poplar. How eagerly we welcomed their return from the south, as they circled our camp like great winged sentinels!

The quiet of the warming days was often broken by the staccato of hungry woodpeckers. Squirrels and later chipmunks visited us for handouts and flicked their tails in salute of our generosity.

One year, two playful weasels came to live in our wood stack and made us laugh with their favorite game. They'd chase each other through the stack and suddenly pop up between the wood sticks. Then, almost before we saw them leave... they were blinking at us from somewhere else. They went so fast that it was like watching six weasels running around in the woodpile.

In the evenings we sat together in the glow of the fire, lost in private worlds of thought. But as the darkness gathered, it seemed to draw us nearer to each other. Families were knit and friendships sealed around the campfire.

Each night, we carried our precious burden of steaming syrup home. Walking down the trail, I felt close to the people who had come to the grove long ago. I could almost see them walking among the trees, peering into catch-cans and nodding in satisfaction. I could almost hear the mud sucking softly at their feet, as they went to warm themselves at our abandoned fire still glowing with bright coals.

The closing of the sugar bush was celebrated with a thanksgiving feast. Then, one by one, we picked up our packs to leave. Single file, we moved down the muddy trail. One by one, we paused at the turn in the path to look back.

The quiet woods, the crisp spring air, the cry of the owl, and the echo of tradition had had their way with us. To ourselves, we promised to return again... when the box-elders begin to weep.

SPRING COMES TO OAK POINT _____

THE REDPOLLS ARRIVED at noon. I heard their hungry chorus and rushed out into the sunny day to welcome them with gifts of sunflower seed.

I managed to get out of the house again about four p.m., but by then the clouds had gathered and the inviting day had become cooler.

Still, I dressed a bit warmer and ventured forth, carrying a bag of sunflower seeds... in case I should be accosted by friendly chickadees while upon my solitary journey.

I stopped to offer a bit of tobacco to a red willow I'd broken on the previous day.

A brisk wind was coming out of the south and grew more intense as I crossed the wide open area near the Unnamed River.

I paused to listen to a busy downy woodpecker tapping for food, while a great aspen creaked painfully. Then I saw the red fruit dried in the tops of the sumac bushes... displaying a dash of color along the road now edged with snirt.

But of the many trees I met today, one appealed to me above all others. A tall, slender sapling birch, growing in the shadow of a jack pine, was bursting from its rose-bronze coat of youth to display the new bark of maturity. It stopped my heart.

Near Phillip's road, I stood to admire the handiwork

of time. Burnt-gold white-pine needles hung in the understory of spruce as delicately as though a gentle hand had placed them there with loving care. The coming winds of March will bring them down... lightly they will slip to the needled forest floor to nourish other nations.

Near my house I saw them. Could I believe my eyes? Yes, several tiny gleaming pussy-willow catkins were nudging from their winter shells!

Back in my own yard, the cheerful chickadees were waiting for seeds still in my pocket.

WHEN EARTH WAS NEW⸺⸺⸺⸺⸺⸺⸺⸺⸺

L ONG, LONG, long ago... when Earth was new, Anishinabe was told by Great Spirit that he must walk the earth and name all the plants, animals, mountains, and lands that had been created.

While Anishinabe went about this task, he noticed the passing of seasons. He saw how all of life was part of the great unending cycle.

The plants received new life in the spring. In the summer, they produced seed for the next generation. The leaves fell to the ground in the fall and returned to enrich Mother Earth. Then winter's cold and snow cleansed the earth. In the spring it all began again.

He went everywhere. There was no place he did not touch.

Anishinabe identified the plants... what was good to eat, what was good for medicine, and what could be used for other purposes. He saw that Earth produced very much food.

He named all the waters. He found that some rivers ran underground... the arteries and veins of Mother Earth. Water cleanses and restores and brings growth. It is life.

He also named the animals and found that each had their own wisdom. He noticed all animals came in pairs and reproduced. Yet, he was alone.

He spoke to Great Spirit, "Why am I alone?"

Great Spirit said, "I will give you a friend."

He sent Wolf.

Anishinabe was pleased and asked Great Spirit, "What more would you have me do?"

Great Spirit said, "Now that you have a friend, you must walk the earth together and visit all the places again."

In this journey, they became more than friends... now they were like brothers.

When it was done, Anishinabe and Wolf sat down and the Great Spirit told them, "Now it is time to go on separate paths. But your way is the same. What happens to one will happen to the other. Each of you will be feared, respected, and misunderstood by the people that will one day share the earth with you."

What Great Spirit said has come to pass.

Both Anishinabe and Wolf mate for life. Both have a tribe and clan system. Both have had their land taken. Both have been hunted for their hair. And both were pushed toward extinction.

But when we look closer at the many things brother Wolf has endured, we can see a better future. We see that Wolf is returning and gaining strength in the places where he was once destroyed.

This teaches us that the Anishinabe people will also return and gain strength in the places where we were destroyed. Perhaps we will lead the way to natural living, teaching the newcomers to respect Mother Earth and live by her perfect laws.

Of course, if we are going to show the way toward that better life, we must first demonstrate that we are ready to live in harmony with all who share earth and honor the plan Great Spirit gave us.

THE THRUSH

L ONG AGO the birds had no song. Only Anishinabe could sing. Every morning Anishinabe sang to greet the new day and the birds perched nearby to listen. Every evening Anishinabe sang to set the sun and the birds listened.

One day the Great Spirit was walking through the fields and forests of the earth. He was disappointed because there was so little music in the land.

The next day he called a council of the birds. When they gathered, the light of the sun was blotted out and the sound of their wings filled the darkness.

"Do you want to sing like Anishinabe?" the Great Spirit asked.

"Yes," the excited birds answered in unison.

"Then you must accomplish a great feat," he told them. "Tomorrow at sunrise you must begin to fly upward. You must fly as high as you possibly can...to reach as close to the sky as your heart and wings will carry you. There you will find your song. Each song will be different. The most beautiful song will be found in the highest reaches of the sky."

The birds were ready for the contest before sunrise. As far as one could see around the council rock were birds of every size and color.

The small brown thrush, with its bright eyes and spotted breast, sat slowly raising and lowering his rust-colored tail as he considered his chances of winning a beautiful song. "How," he asked himself, "can I win with such small wings?"

He watched the great golden eagle preening nearby and an idea came to him. Quickly the thrush hid himself under the feathers of the large bird.

The eagle was thinking, "I am certain to win the most beautiful song, for my powerful wings will carry me higher than any other bird."

Finally the red sun rose over the horizon and the birds leaped skyward. They beat their wings rapidly against the constant pull of the earth.

Higher and higher they climbed. Soon the weaker birds tired and dropped back to earth. The small low-flying birds had simple songs. Some returned with only one note which they repeated again and again.

At sunset only a few birds still flew upward and as the sun rose again only the great golden eagle remained in the sky.

But now his mighty wings grew heavy and beat more weakly. As the eagle was reaching his peak, the thrush flew out of his hiding place. The eagle saw the thrush and began to pursue the small bird. But the great wings could not lift him any higher and with an angry cry, the eagle began his descent.

As the eagle came down, the thrush went up. He flew joyfully onward and found himself in the spirit world, where he heard the most beautiful song of all.

He stayed there until he had mastered the heavenly music. Then he left to return to the earth.

But it was a long way back, and the little bird had time to think of how unfair it had been of him to cheat the eagle out of his song. He was so ashamed that he did not return to the council rock where the other birds waited.

Instead, he flew away to the dense woodlands of the north and hid himself among the bushes. Today he still hides deep in the forest and that is why he is called the hermit thrush.

Because he is ashamed of how he won his song, he seldom sings. But when he raises his beautiful voice to sing his flute-like song, other birds perch nearby and listen to the wonderful music that the lonely thrush brought back from the spirit world.

THE LITTLE BEINGS _____

HISTORICALLY, "little beings" have been seen in the Red Lake and White Earth woodlands. My great aunt, Rose Downwind, told me that she had seen them several times during her life. She said they would quickly hide from her by jumping into the water or disappearing into small holes in the ground.

My mother, Maefred Vanoss Arey, told me that "little spirits of the woodlands" have always enjoyed helping young children. Therefore, children must be trained to watch for and give heed to them. She said if danger is before a child, the spirit will break a stick and throw it down in the child's path as a warning. Such spirits are quite friendly and act as guardians.

These spirits also live in the waters. The "little water beings" are quite shy but they have power to calm stormy waters. These little ones help people to travel safely over lakes and rivers. Although the Anishinabe have great respect for these beings, they were never worshipped or considered to be gods.

In the long ago, when the people were plagued by small troubles, they often blamed it on the little beings, but it was usually the mischief of Wanabozho. Although Wanabozho is often portrayed as a hero in Anishinabe stories, he was much like other men. He enjoyed a good joke and tricked the people for fun... but he could be tricked, too.

When the Anishinabe offered gifts to the little spirits of the woodlands or of the water, they did not do it because they thought the spirits were angry. The gifts were to thank them for their help or to ask for additional assistance. The people believed that these spirits wanted to be helpful.

At one time, these little beings could understand the people by reading their thoughts. Unfortunately, except for a few young children, most Anishinabe no longer think or speak or act in that spiritual realm.

Therefore, not everyone can see the little beings because they only show themselves to persons of the most excellent character. Such people are highly sensitive and of an exceptionally kind and generous personality.

Although the little beings of today are very careful to avoid contact with nearly all people, there is still one reliable means of contacting them.

In early spring, you must go into the forest and search for the plant called "jack-in-the-pulpit." Then... on your knees, with your mouth held close to Jack's green hood, and speaking in the softest whisper... you can leave a message for the little people. This is the only time during the cycle of the earth's seasons that the plant will hold a message.

As in the past, you may ask for help with a particular problem or you may express gratitude for kindnesses you have already received. But if you are wise... you will not make a selfish request! Little beings will not listen to such talk.

Nor will they listen to whining complaints or gossip. They simply don't have time for such unproductive nonsense.

I have several grandchildren now, and leaving secrets for the little people has become a spring ritual for us. It's so exciting to know that little beings will come and coax your secrets from the hooded plants.

I can almost see it. The little being stepping close... with a delicate hand cupped over a tiny ear, the small face crinkled with a smile and the elfish head nodding approval....

Please don't miss your chance to share a secret with the little people. I know I won't.

RABBIT AND OTTER _____

ONE DAY RABBIT went to visit his very good friend, Otter.

"Otter," said Rabbit, "let us go camping down by the river."

"But," Otter worried, "I've never been anywhere. I might get lost! Furthermore, I've never even seen the river. I can't swim. I might drown!"

"Come on," Rabbit persuaded. "I've been everywhere. You won't get lost if you follow me. And you don't have to swim, if you don't want to."

So Otter agreed to go with Rabbit. When they reached the river they set up their camp. After they'd eaten, Rabbit said, "Let's play a game."

"No," Otter replied. "I don't play games."

"Well," Rabbit suggested, "should we dance?"

"I don't dance, either," said Otter.

"Well," Rabbit wanted to know, "what do you do for fun?"

"Oh," whined Otter, "I don't have any fun."

"Of course not," snapped Rabbit, "you don't even try!"

Now Rabbit had always been a bit jealous of Otter because he had such a fine coat. So he decided to have his own kind of fun... at Otter's expense.

"I'll have fun... even if he doesn't," Rabbit chuckled to himself.

"Otter," he whispered, "do you know where we are?"

"You know I don't," Otter replied.

"Well," Rabbit began, "this is called 'where fire falls from the sky.' It has been said that on cool, starry nights... like this is... when the wind sighs gently through the pines... as it's doing now... and the water flows south... as you see it is flowing at this time... it might happen on such a night that the fire of legend will fall."

"Well," cried Otter, "I want to go home!"

"But," Rabbit quickly continued, "we will sleep close to the river. If fire falls, I'll warn you... then you jump into the river so you won't get any holes in your beautiful coat."

So Otter and Rabbit lay down close to the water. When Rabbit was sure that Otter was sleeping, he took a piece of bark and, with it, scooped up the coals from the fire. He tossed them up into the air and screamed, "The fire is falling!"

Otter moved like lightening and hit the water as the glowing coals came down. Then, before he knew what had happened... he was swimming!

From that day to this, Otter chooses to live close to the water. He often praises his good friend Rabbit.

"Yes," Otter likes to say, "it was Rabbit who taught me to appreciate the pleasures of life. Didn't he take me camping? Didn't he teach me to swim? Surely no one ever had a friend as kind as he."

Rabbit is greatly annoyed by such gracious praise

but Otter doesn't seem to notice.

Now, Otter has more fun than Rabbit, and when you see Otter sitting quietly on the river bank or swimming along on his back, you will notice that he always smiles a little.

Do you suppose Otter has had the last laugh after all?

IT HAPPENED in the long, long ago that there was a nation of troubled people. They were troubled by vexing spirits. Some of these spirits were as small as fleas, others as large as deerflies. They say that a few were as big as the great moose.

Now, all these spirits lived in the land of "Look-Behind." It was called by this name because the spirits were always sneaking up behind the unhappy people who lived there.

Then the leaders of these people said that everyone should walk backwards so they could see the spirits that buzzed about, stinging them and biting them, causing infection, sores, and diseases. But no matter which way the people walked... the spirits were always behind them.

So some of the bold warriors, who wore proud courage feathers, made horrible masks to wear on the back of their heads. They were sure that now the spirits could not tell if the two-faced men were coming or going.

But this did not help. In fact, it made things worse. You see, these spirits could not be fooled, but they could be annoyed. Soon, they became irritated and angry. To show their displeasure, they put an eternal curse upon such people. Because of this... from that day to this day... and even beyond tomorrow... no one will ever be able to trust any two-faced person.

At last, the troubled people of Look-Behind decided to hold a great council meeting. The medicine men built the council fire of pine heartwood and kindled it with the youngest flame struck from the sacred flint.

They sprinkled the fire with tobacco and fed it with the eyes of a lynx, the tail of a beaver, and the brain of a fox. They did this so that they could see clearly what must be done to keep the spirits from harassing them, to help them be strong in their resolve, and so that they might think cunning thoughts.

The smoke hazed up and billowed out and grew up into a thick black cloud that covered the people of Look-Behind, shutting them up in darkness. This was a terrible experience for the pitiful people. Of course, they were frightened.

But out of the cloud came Father Water, a sad and gentle giant. They say he was so big that no one had ever seen all of him at the same time.

In a voice as soft as the whisper of the wind, he spoke to the poor people crouched around the fire. He told them not to fear the vexing spirits of Look-Behind. He told them that he would trap the spirits in lakes that he would scatter across the land. He told them that every lake would catch the spirits that wanted to torment the people.

He said, "These lakes will be filled with water from my own body. Then I must lie down and die. It is my wish that you and your people should care for my body forever. But it is for you and you alone to know that my heart-place will be a shallow lake." Then he disappeared, the council fire flickered out, the smoke lifted, and the darkness was gone.

Now the people could see clearly. They had new confidence and were able to understand many things that had puzzled them before.

Now they looked out upon a new land of great beauty. The land was dotted with sparkling lakes, and through the land ran a mighty river, full of strength and abounding with life. They called the river "Father of Waters." Today it is called the Mississippi.

The people traveled down the river and found the shallow place that Father Water called his heart-place. This is now called Lake Pepin.

The people chose this place for mourning and burying their dead. It is said that for hundreds of years they wrapped their dead in birchbark and took them down the river to burial sites along Lake Pepin.

They did this so they could be certain that their loved ones would lie forever in the heart-place of Father Water. They knew that as long as the people remembered to honor him, they would continue to live long and pleasant lives in a good land.

For countless generations, the children were carefully instructed to respect the river. But now the great river is dying, and we who were charged to care for it seem powerless to prevent it. Others are apathetic, unmoved by the plight we have brought upon ourselves by failing to respect the river and forgetting to honor Father Water.

Because we are no longer ignorant of the great harm that has been done to this mighty river... this gift from Father Water... we will pay a price. People all along the river will pay; our children and our grandchildren will pay.

We see Father Water lying in his bed corrupted and defiled by those who exploit our resources. It is as though the purpose of the river is only to serve the careless, the ignorant, the unprincipled and greedy.

Surely this cannot be allowed to continue. Surely we have some leaders who can still see clearly, who understand what must be done, and who have the courage to stand up in defense of Father Water and declare, "Enough! It is enough! Stop destroying our river."

It is time to let the river heal. It is time to honor Father Water just as the Old Ones did.

It is time to free Father Water from the pollution and contaminants that trouble our great river... just as Father Water freed the people from the spirits that troubled them in the long ago land of Look-Behind.

If we need encouragement to find the strength to stand in defense of Turtle Island and the Mississippi River, perhaps we should turn to Fisher for an example of perseverance and self-sacrifice.

L ONG AGO... when the earth was rich with life, the water was clean, and the air was clear, all the animals were friends and spoke a common language. Because they were friends and spoke a common language, they often gathered to celebrate great and small events.

It was during such a celebration that Bear looked up into the sky and saw a strange thing.

"Look," he cried. "A dark robe is falling over the day star!"

Then all the animals looked up and saw that it was so. Within seconds, darkness covered the sun and engulfed the earth. Nothing like this had ever happened before. The animals were frightened and confused.

"Something must be done," said Bear.

So the great animals gathered at the council hill and held a conference to discuss what they should do.

Already the darkness was growing cold, and the tender plants had begun to wither. The small animals waited for the great animals to do something. They waited and waited... and while they waited, the great ones went on talking and talking... and talking.

At last, Fisher came forward to address the council. "Let me help," he pleaded.

But Bear, who was very kind, said, "Oh, Fisher. You're too small. There's nothing you can do. Such a great problem can only be resolved by the great ones... and we are the great ones."

So Fisher went away.

At last, the great ones decided that Bear should go to the top of the high council hill and see what he could do about the darkness.

So Bear climbed to the top of the hill, raised up to his full height and, growling fiercely, slashed at the darkness with his great black claws.

But it was no use. It was still dark. So Bear returned to the conference, and the great ones went on talking.

Again Fisher came forward. "Please, let me try to help," he said.

But Deer, who was very patient, said, "No, Fisher You're too small. This is a great problem. Such a problem can only be solved by the great ones and we are the great ones."

So Fisher went away.

At last, the great ones decided that Deer should go to the top of the high council hill and see what he could do about the darkness.

So Deer climbed to the top of the hill, stood on his back legs, shook his great antlers, and ripped at the darkness with his sharp hooves.

But it was no use. It was still dark. So Deer returned to the council meeting of the great ones, and the great ones went on talking.

For a third time, Fisher came forward. "Please, let me try," he said.

But Mountain Lion, who was not as kind as Bear or as patient as Deer, said, "Fisher, I'm tired of your silly talk. This is a serious matter we are discussing and your interruptions are not helpful. You're too small! So stop your foolish chatter and go away."

So Fisher went away.

Then it was decided that Mountain Lion should go to the top of the high council hill and see what he could do about the darkness.

So Mountain Lion climbed to the top of the hill, leaped into the sky, snarled viciously, and tore at the darkness with his mighty claws.

But it was no use. It was still dark. So Mountain Lion returned to the council meeting, and the great ones went on talking.

Once more, Fisher came forward. "Please, let me try. I only want to help," he begged.

Before anyone could speak, Bear said, "Very well, Fisher. You may try. Truly, the great ones have been unable to solve the problem."

So Fisher ran to the top of the hill and leaped into the sky, pulling at the darkness with his small paws.

But it was no use. It changed nothing and the darkness prevailed. So Fisher leaped into the sky again and again, and again and again he fell back to the earth. All his efforts changed nothing.

At last Bear said, "Oh, Fisher! Please stop! You're hurting yourself!"

But Fisher did not seem to hear Bear.

Instead he ran to the bottom of the hill and lay down to rest. As he lay there, he prayed. "Oh, Great Spirit, help me run up this hill faster than I have ever run before. Help me to leap higher than anyone has ever leaped before. Help me bring light back to our earth."

Then he ran up the hill faster than he had ever run before. Then he leaped higher than anyone had ever leaped before. Then... he touched the darkness with his small paws and fell back to earth.

To the joy of all the animals, the darkness fell away from the face of the day star, and light filled the sky and covered the earth.

Such an event was surely worthy of a celebration! So the animals began to sing and dance, and the great ones made long, loud, proud speeches.

At last Bear said, "We must honor Fisher, for it was Fisher who prevailed against the darkness and restored light to the day star."

"Come forward, Fisher," Deer called.

But Fisher did not come forward and no one could find him.

Then Bear remembered that he hadn't seen Fisher since he'd fallen back to earth on the high council hill. So he hurried up the hill, followed by all the other animals.

They found Fisher... but he was dead.

So they gathered around his small broken body and mourned his death.

Great Spirit heard the sound of their grieving and

came to the council hill. Gently, Great Spirit lifted Fisher and carried him up into the sky. Great Spirit placed Fisher in the northern part of heaven and marked the place with a star.

Then Great Spirit returned to the council and told the animals this: "When you go out at night, you will see Fisher's star shining in the north. You will call it the "home star" because this is the star that will guide you home. And when you see Fisher's star shining in the north, remember... Fisher was not a great one! Indeed, he was very small. Remember this, too. Remember that, although he was small, it was he who prevailed against the darkness and brought light back to our cold, dark, dying earth."

FIREFLY WATCH _____

I WAS JUST FINISHING my evening shower when John tapped on the bathroom door.

"The meadow is full of fireflies," he said. "Want to walk over and watch them for awhile?"

"No," I answered, "not tonight."

Within minutes, I'd changed my mind. I did not want to miss an opportunity to see the wide meadow fill with a multitude of small blinking miracles. Quickly I pulled on my white robe, tied on my sneakers, and ran down our rut-road.

I saw John through the light fog. Just as I was about to call, he turned and let out an awful yell. Without looking back, I ran as fast as I could and caught up to him.

When I turned to see what had frightened him... I saw that we were alone.

"Boy," I said, "you sure scared me!"

"Well, how do you think I felt?" he returned. "You looked like a ghost flapping through the night!"

We laughed so hard we could barely stand up. Then we continued our walk through the friendly darkness.

The fireflies had gathered over the whole meadow, floating three to four feet above the ground. It was like a gentle lake, glowing mysteriously with a million tiny beacons.

Oh, what a treasure of pleasure we found on our firefly watch!

FROM THE FOURTH HILL of my elderhood, I recall many things and I see them more clearly.

I remember when, as a young mother, I was blessed with six beautiful children. Oh, how I pitied all the other mothers who had to pretend that their children were beautiful. It was only yesterday that I realized all young mothers probably feel the same way about their children, and it was only today that I could laugh at my foolishness.

Climbing the fourth hill, I find that I greatly enjoy the friendship of my adult children. When the silence between us is as comfortable as an old sweatshirt, I remember the wisdom of Oneida writer and friend, Roberta Hill Whiteman. In the deep respectful silence, we can pause together... like kindred spirits... and listen to the "snow inside the moon."

Sometimes my daughters are mirrors and I look at myself in them. Sometimes I think they find themselves in me.

My sons make me smile at the old notion that it was I who was strong as a tree and they who came to me for life. Now it is clear that I am not strong, and my sons are like stout trees bringing life and strength to me.

CHARLIE'S BEANS _____

THE NEIGHBORHOOD children had chosen sides for a softball game but no one wanted Charlie on their team. Even his two older brothers didn't want him to play.

"You're just too small to play," said Steven.

"You can't run," said Tom.

Charlie wandered into our small garden. "Mom, can I help you?" he asked.

I looked toward the sunny field where the softball players were taking their positions. "Oh, Charlie," I said, "I really need help with the beans. Can you be in charge of them?"

"Sure, Mom," he beamed.

Charlie listened carefully to my instructions. Soon he'd dug a shallow L-shaped trench along two sides of the garden.

I cut a stick four inches long and showed Charlie how to space the beans. Then I cut a notch in one end of the stick to show him how deep to plant the beans. "They should be about four inches apart and one inch deep," I explained.

Charlie did just as he was told. If the trench was too deep, he added dirt. If the trench was too shallow, he scooped dirt out. Then he laid the beans in the trench, and I inspected his work.

"Well done!" I shouted with proud enthusiasm.

Then, on my knees, I showed Charlie how to cover the beans. Carefully he refilled the trench and pressed the cool, damp soil down firmly with his hand.

When he finished, I gave him a small package of marigold seeds. "They look like fat eyelashes," he commented.

"They sure do!" I laughed.

"But," Charlie wanted to know, "why are we planting flowers in our vegetable garden?"

"The marigolds will keep the bean beetles from spoiling our vegetables," I told him.

Taking his hand, I showed him how to poke small finger-holes here and there along the row of beans. "Only this deep," I said, holding his thumb against his finger. "If the seeds are buried too deeply they won't grow, and we need marigold soldiers to protect our garden."

After the marigolds were planted, Charlie and I stood together quietly looking at our garden. In my eyes, it was full of vegetables and as good as harvested. Charlie saw nothing but dirt.

Every day he looked for some sign that the beans were growing. By the end of the week, he'd become quite discouraged. "Maybe the beans won't grow," he said one morning.

"I'll bet they're growing right now," I said. Pulling on my old red sweater I hurried toward the garden.

Charlie followed with dragging steps.

I stooped down and carefully picked at the dirt near

the end of the fence. Soon I'd uncovered a sprouted bean and laid it in Charlie's hand. His eyes grew bright with new excitement.

He showed it to Tom. "Wow!" said Tom, hooking his thumbs over his belt.

He showed it to Steven. "Hmmm," said Steven, raising one eyebrow.

Tom wanted to show it to Arnie.

Steve wanted to show it to Paul.

Charlie wanted to show it to everyone.

By the end of the second week, tiny green-bean plants were peeking out of the earth. They stood in a straight row along the edge of the rusty wire fence. I showed Charlie how to curl the tender vines around the wire to help them climb the fence.

The lacy green foliage of the marigold army had also grown up. I showed Charlie how to thin the plants. "Pinch off the plants that don't get off to a good start," I said. "Thinning is important... it helps the healthy plants get the food and water they need to grow."

One day, Charlie noticed the bean buds. Soon the buds opened and the pale pink petals of the bean blossoms unfolded. Then the garden was visited by busy bees and butterflies.

"Don't frighten the bees," Charlie warned Steven. "They're pollinating the vegetables."

Together, they watched a fuzzy bee buzz from one flower to another as it gathered nectar to take back to its hive.

When I hoed between the rows, Charlie pulled weeds. He was careful not to disturb the vegetable roots. Steven and Tom helped keep the garden watered when it didn't rain.

Suddenly, thin velvety beans hung on the strong vines. Charlie watched them grow long and thick. When they were as big as my finger, I said, "It's time to start picking beans, Charlie."

"Can I help?" asked Tom.

"Sure," said Charlie. He showed Tom how to hold the vine with one hand and pluck the bean off with the other. "If you pull them like this," he explained, "you won't hurt the vines."

Soon I was cooking beans for supper three times a week and canning several pints a day.

The boys picked beans for Grandma Arey, too.

"What lovely beans," she commented. "Where did you get them?"

"Charlie raised them," Steven told her. "He's a bean expert."

Soon Grandma's freezer was full of beans.

Charlie picked beans every day and the beans kept growing.

The neighborhood children noticed the beans, too. Charlie picked beans for them to take home.

Charlie was getting pretty tired of beans when an early frost brought the harvest to an end.

But now it was time for football.

Steven said, "We need someone to hold the ball when we kick."

Raising one eyebrow, Charlie said, "I can do that."

Tom said, "We need a good referee."

The little bean-expert hooked his thumbs over his belt and said, "I can do that, too."

F OX HAD BECOME very sick from something he had eaten and he lay down to die. He was in great pain when Mouse came along.

"Why do you lie here as one who is dying?" Mouse asked.

"Because I am dying," groaned Fox. "I'm too sick to reach the good greens that will cleanse this poison from my body."

Mouse said, "Tell me what to do. I will help you."

Fox told Mouse where to go and what to look for. Then Mouse scampered off.

After awhile Mouse returned with the greens. Fox ate them and in a few minutes he was able to stand.

"Thank you, my small friend," Fox said. "I will never forget what you have done. I will tell all my relatives. We will remember forever. This is my promise."

By and by Mouse came upon a blind wolf.

"Help me!" Wolf cried. "I must get to the clear water that runs in a shallow stream near the edge of the forest. Then I can wash the infection from my eyes. Then I will see again. Please help me."

Mouse said, "I will lead the way. Follow the sound of my voice."

So Mouse led Wolf to the shallow stream. Wolf washed his eyes and soon he could see well enough.

"Thank you, my small friend," said Wolf. "I will never

forget what you have done. I will tell all my relatives. We will remember forever. This is my promise."

By and by Mouse came upon Eagle, who had a snare around his neck. Eagle was gasping for air and was unable to move.

"Help me," croaked the great bird.

Quickly Mouse chewed through the snare and set Eagle free.

When Eagle was able to breathe, he said, "Thank you, my small friend. I will never forget what you have done today. I will tell all my relatives. We will remember forever. This is my promise."

So Mouse went on his way. He led a safe, happy life and raised many children. He often told his family how he'd saved Fox, Wolf, and Eagle from certain death. He repeated the promise each had given him.

When Mouse was very old... he died.

"Remember," he said in the end, "we have nothing to fear. We have the promise. Fox, Wolf, and Eagle have said that our relatives will always be friends."

But after Old Mouse died, the children of Fox violated their father's promise and began to eat Mouse's children. Wolf's children also began to eat mice. Eagle's did likewise. And so mice were hunted, killed, and eaten by their former friends.

The promise was no longer spoken of and soon it was completely forgotten.

UNCLE'S CAMERA _____

It's just an old camera, a survivor, you see.
My uncle carried it over the sea.
It was there with him at Normandy.

It's big as a book with stories to tell.
It told us of friendships forgotten in hell,
Of great wasted cities and battles to quell.

Of waist-deep water in fear and chills,
Of frantic runs up strategic hills,
Of body bags and counted kills.

He closed the eye with bellows fold,
But still he saw the war of old,
On films of dreams and mem'ries rolled.

In alcohol he lived to find
A deep sweet calm for his troubled mind,
And left the beaches far behind.

"He fell," they said... and soon he died.
The bugle called... he left with pride.
I held his hand while Mama cried.

The camera lay in a leather case
With photos nothing could erase,
Of youthful smile and jaunty grace.

Softly he whispered, when he was but three,
"Mama, will you always take care of me?"
He wept for the children when he was but four,
"What is the reason that people make war?"

So we pray for the children, for my child and yours,
Mothers of brothers on both sides of wars.

"Mama," he asked me, when he was but nine,
"Will I have to die in Vietnam?"
I lied when I told him, with tears in my eyes,
"This war will end and men will grow wise."

Now we pray for the children, for my child and yours,
Mothers of brothers on both sides of wars.

I hear his voice as he calls 'cross the land,
"Someone is hurting me, please hold my hand.
Mama, I wish now that I was but three,
Safe in your arms, like I used to be."

Let us pray for the children, for my child and yours,
Mothers of brothers on both sides of wars.

SAME-SAME

IT HAPPENED in Vietnam during the early '60s, but like so many memories, it seems to grow more vivid with the years.

He was a young American Indian serving in the U.S. Army. Of the South Vietnamese, he said, "They could have been neighbors from my home reservation."

He told of being pinned down by a North Vietnamese for a day and a night.

"I saw him, and he saw me. We took aim on each other. But neither one of us fired. We watched each other for the rest of the day. I stayed there all night. In the morning he was gone."

But it was an old Vietnamese village woman who put it into words. She saw him during a patrol and came forward. She held her arm against his. With the other hand, she plucked at his skin.

Smiling up at him, she said, "You same-same."

The Hopi tell of the "children's fire."

It is said that the children's fire must forever be guarded by the elders... the grandparents.

How do we guard the children's fire? By standing alone in difficult places to give the children of tomorrow a good life in a good land.

Like many people today, I have often wondered what kind of a world we are leaving to our grandchildren.

In the beginning there was the land... seemingly endless stands of white and red pine, innumerable streams and sparkling lakes... and there were the people of the land, the Anishinabe.

The Anishinabe were told by Great Spirit to be the caretakers of this land. The people lived by the philosophy that the Earth, Water, and Sky did not belong to the two-legged residents. They believed that Earth, Sky, and Water must be protected.

The Anishinabe believed that the needs of the next seven generations should be considered before all things... that no single generation should be allowed to deny the next generation the same opportunities and blessings that had been enjoyed by the previous seven.

For thousands of years, our ancestors took care that the resources were not exploited. However, that position of stewardship was usurped by the European invaders.

The great forests are gone now, plundered for profit.

The streams and lakes are under siege. The people of the land are now standing at the end of a dismal history. Poised and expectant... they await the season of respect and restitution. They await a new and honorable history that can be written with dignity and truth.

From the fourth hill of my elderhood, I see the children's fire... and I am troubled.

But I also see a quiet movement of reconciliation which includes all nations gathering at the fire. Soon we will learn to dance.

SONG OF RECONCILIATION

All the battles legend-long
still lie about us.
Weapons at hand,
we stand.

Spread now your pale hands
toward the warmth of my small fire.

Gather now my robe
around your thin shoulders.

Dip now your dry bread
into my soup.

Take now your stick
to strike my broken drum.

When you hear my song,
we will dance.

SUMMER

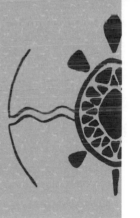

SUMMER

MUSKRAT'S TAIL

IN THE DAYS of long ago, Muskrat had a long, bushy tail. He was so proud of his tail that he combed it every morning and brushed it every night. He even made up songs about it, which he sang grandly as he groomed his beautiful tail.

Now Rabbit, who had a very little tail, was jealous of Muskrat and decided to play a trick on him.

It was Rabbit's duty to invite all the animals to an important celebration. So he went to Muskrat's house to talk with him about the great event.

"Will you come to the dance?" Rabbit asked.

"Yes," Muskrat answered. "I certainly will go to the dance if I can sit in a place of honor where everyone can admire my wonderful tail."

Rabbit said, "I will be happy to arrange it. I will also send two elder mice to your home the night before the event. They will wash and brush your tail until it shines. Then they will wrap it in sweet-grass to keep it clean. Not only will your tail be wonderful to see, but it will be a joy to smell."

This pleased Muskrat very much and he spent the rest of the day composing a new song about his lovely tail. He planned to sing and dance at the celebration.

Then Rabbit went to the home of the two old mice.

"It will be your job to groom Muskrat's tail for the dance," he told them. "You will go to his house the night before the event. You will wash and brush his tail. Then you will rub him between the eyes until he falls asleep. While he is sleeping, you will chew all the hair off his tail with your sharp teeth. Then wrap the tail in long blades of sweet-grass."

So the mice went to Muskrat's house and did as Rabbit had told them. The next day, Muskrat went to the dance. He took his place of honor and began to sing his tail-song.

Carefully he danced, loosening the sweet-grass wrap with each step. Muskrat was deeply satisfied and closed his eyes in ecstasy. When all the grass had dropped off his tail, he danced more proudly. He moved around the circle holding his tail up for all to see.

Everyone shouted, "Look at Muskrat's tail!"

Muskrat was pleased. He danced around the circle

again, holding his tail higher.

Suddenly everyone was laughing! Muskrat opened his eyes to see what was so funny. He saw that they were laughing at him!

He looked up at his beautiful tail... there was no hair on it! It was a black ugly rope of flesh. Muskrat was so ashamed that he ran away and hid himself in the river.

Now, Muskrat and his grandchildren still hide in the river. But sometimes... when the moon shines softly on the water, Muskrat comes up out of the river to sit on a little hump of mud. Then, alone in the night, he sings... sad, quiet little songs about the beautiful tail that was lost.

Lost... because of Muskrat pride... and Rabbit jealousy.

FIRE

THERE WAS A TIME when the Anishinabe did not know how to make fire.

They knew there was a nation far away that had learned how to make fire. However, that nation did not share their knowledge with others because it gave them great power.

The knowledge of making fire had made that nation strong, and they used it against their relatives. They had invented many instruments of war and overwhelmed their peaceful neighbors.

So it happened one day that the Anishinabe decided that they needed fire, too. A young man was selected to go to that far-away nation and bring back the knowledge of making fire. He was carefully chosen, for such a man must be strong and brave, cunning and wise.

Soon he was on his way. It was a long, difficult journey, but at last he reached the land of the fire-people. Now, he knew that since the strong nation did not choose to share their fire-making skills, he would have to find some cunning way to get the knowledge his people needed.

So he waited in a hidden place and observed how the people built a fire. He saw that they had strange, black, wonderful spark-throwing stones. This was what he needed. He would have to get into the camp and take one of the stones.

At last, he saw an opportunity. Bravely he walked into the camp and took a stone that had been left lying near a new fire.

Then, with the prize in his hand... he ran. Of course he was pursued, but his strong legs carried him quickly away and no one was able to catch him. He was able even to escape their mighty weapons.

At last, he entered his village. Of course he was greeted with a hero's welcome and a feast. The happy people celebrated their new knowledge and how powerful it would make them.

Then the young man built a great fire and invited all the nations that did not have the knowledge of making fire to come and take a coal.

When his people murmured against what he did, he reminded them, "I was chosen not only for my cunning, bravery, and strength, but also for my wisdom."

The people realized that he was right, and they decided that they must trust in his wisdom... just as they had trusted in his cunning, bravery, and strength.

From that day forth, all people had equal power and, for many years, war was no more than a memory.

The generous man shared the fire and with it, the power that it gave two-leggeds. Brother Beaver is also honored for his generosity. But once again, we see what jealousy will do to a nation.

WHEN BEAVER WAS VERY GREAT_____

IT HAPPENED in the long, long ago that Beaver was very great. He walked upright and stood as tall as the tallest man. Furthermore, Beaver was highly intelligent and deeply spiritual.

Beaver had the ability to improve his environment and make it more hospitable for many other animals, too.

Beaver established communities of families that worked together to build great earthen lodges. The lodges were so well constructed that Beaver did not have to gather wood for fires to heat the lodges.

Beaver did not have to make robes or clothing of any kind because they were blessed with fur-covered bodies.

Beaver had wonderful long sharp teeth which allowed them to fell large trees with ease. Beaver often cut trees for their human neighbors... whom Beaver had grown to pity. In exchange, Beaver asked only for the tender bark and twigs to store for winter food.

During warm weather, Beaver probed the bottom of lakes and rivers for roots and relished many kinds of greens.

Beaver made long canals and built fine roads throughout their territory which made transport and travel easier. They shared the canals and roadways with their neighbors.

The Anishinabe learned many good things by observing Beaver.

Beaver bathed several times a day. Soon, people adopted these habits of cleanliness and good grooming practices.

Beaver were excellent parents and raised respectful, industrious children. So the Anishinabe imitated Beaver's parenting skills.

Beaver worked hard to accomplish good deeds that would benefit the entire community. They did not quarrel and fight among themselves and did not make enemies of their neighbors. They experienced no jealousy when others excelled.

Therefore, as time went on... Beaver prospered more than people.

So a delegation of men went to Creator and reminded him that he had promised that they would be the greatest of all created beings. Then they pointed out that Beaver had surpassed people in many things.

The people demanded that Creator do something to restore their original role and reduce the status and power of Beaver.

Creator said, "If people need an advantage over Beaver in order to surpass him, I will limit Beaver's stature and cause him to desire to live only in and on the water."

The delegates were satisfied and returned to their lodges.

Beaver did not diminish all at once, but each generation became smaller than the one before, and after many years they have become the Beaver we know today.

But Creator allowed Beaver to retain all of their previous skills. They are still intelligent, industrious, and generous. They still work together to modify their habitat and build secure lodges which they share with extended families.

They are still affectionate, considerate, and kind. They do not fight and quarrel among themselves and have only a few enemies.

Beaver's greatest enemy is Man. Man... who learned so many things from our little brother, but failed to learn the important lesson of building inclusive communities.

Because of Beaver's character and former greatness, the Anishinabe believe that they are still worthy of great respect. Therefore, it is dishonorable to allow a dog to eat Beaver flesh, for the dog has never been as great as Beaver... nor can it ever be.

THE STONE CARVER _____

I T WAS A WARM DAY and the heat felt good to the old man. He sat at his workbench but did not work. He closed his tired eyes and held his wrinkled face toward the sun.

A young boy stood nearby. He looked at the deep lines in the old man's dark skin, the soiled shirt hanging from thin shoulders, and the sharp knees that poked against the baggy pants.

His bright eyes saw the tumble of rough pipestone on the ground and the shiny tools laid on the dusty bench.

When the boy looked up, he saw the old man watching him. They smiled together.

The man pointed to a piece of stone, and the boy picked it up.

"What do you see in the stone?" the old man asked.

The boy examined the red stone closely, turning it over and over in careful hands. At last he placed it in the old man's hand. "I see only a stone," he whispered.

Smiling, the old man said, "I see a turtle."

Then, picking up the knife, he began to carve. The bright blade moved quickly, as a pile of soft red dust grew slowly on the ground between his feet. He did not speak again and did not seem to notice when the boy left.

Several days later, the boy thought of the man and

the formless red stone. He remembered what the man had said and he wanted to see the stone again.

The man was seated at his workbench holding the carved turtle when the boy arrived. He touched the boy's shiny nose with a red-stained finger, then rubbed the skin-oil into the stone. He pressed the stone against his own brow and showed the boy how skin-oil enhanced the patterns swirling in the stone.

Then he placed the turtle in the boy's hand, and they smiled together.

The boy turned the turtle over and over as his thin fingers explored every surface and traced every line.

"Yes," he told himself, "a turtle was hidden in the pipestone."

When he looked up, the old man took the turtle. Handing him a knife, the old man said, "There is a wolf in the stone at your feet."

The boy picked up the stone and as he turned it over, he saw a young wolf caught in it. He took the knife and carefully he began to carve. He watched the fine red dust slide across the bright blade. He looked at his red-stained hands. He wondered how many stones he would carve before he became an old man holding his face toward the sun.

SONG OF THE WILD HORSE

THERE WAS A TIME when a man's status was determined by how many horses he had, how well his wife respected him, and the character of his children.

Blue Crane was such a man. He had many fine horses and was greatly honored by his family and his friends.

But over the long years, there were fewer and fewer wild horses until the day came when there were none. No one was too concerned as there were many horses in captivity.

However, when the captive horses stopped reproducing, the people knew that eventually there would be no more horses.

The head man called a council to discuss the situation. Because of his previous success in breeding horses, Blue Crane was asked to speak. He told the people that although he had fasted and prayed over the matter, he did not know what could be done.

There seemed to be no hope.

One day, Blue Crane's youngest son told his father, "I will have fine horses. I'll be just like you one day!"

Blue Crane said, "Soon there will be no more horses."

But the boy insisted. "I had a dream! In the dream I stood on a large stone. I sang the song of the wild horse and they came to me."

"That is a good dream," his father said wearily. "Perhaps it will come to pass."

But the child's dream was soon forgotten.

Then one day, while the boy was hunting small game, he came upon a thick tangle of vines. "I've seen this place before," he whispered in astonishment.

He pushed himself against the vines and after some struggle, broke out on the other side. There he saw the large stone and with great difficulty, he climbed to the top and sang the song of the wild horse.

He sang for three days and three nights.

It happened on the third night, when he was weak with hunger, that he sang his most powerful song.

Suddenly the stone began to shake and a thundering roar rose up around it. Of course the boy was frightened, but he went on singing.

Lightening burst from the dark clouds above him, and great flapping birds tried to knock him off the rock. But he raised his arms and went on singing.

Suddenly a great fiery ball came tumbling toward him above the treetops. He was still singing when it bowled him over.

When he opened his eyes, it was morning. He lay on the stone, too exhausted to move.

Then he heard a soft whinny, and looking over the edge of the stone, he saw three white horses.

He rubbed his eyes and looked again. He saw three white horses and seven black ones.

Once more he rubbed his eyes in disbelief. When

he opened them, he counted twenty-two horses... three white, seven black, and twelve spotted.

He thanked Great Spirit for preserving his life, for sending him the sacred dream, and for the gift of the wild horses. Then he mounted a white one and rode home. The rest of the horses followed.

It was a happy mother that embraced her child that day, and a grateful father who received his son back as though from death.

The village held a feast of thanksgiving for his safe return and for the horses he brought. He was renamed... Little Wild Horse.

Now the captive horses began to reproduce and things went well for the people.

Then one day, Wild Horse set his horses free. But it is said that whenever he sang their song, they returned just as strong and wonderful as they were on the day he first saw them.

Still, a man's life is brief at last, so Wild Horse grew old and passed on. Now there was no one who could sing the song that brought the horses back to the people.

Yet, there are those who say they have seen a herd of phantom horses running silently under moonlit skies.

Perhaps they are looking for Little Wild Horse. Or perhaps they seek another child of courage and power who can sing them back to the physical world.

THE TROPHY

THE LONG-AWAITED summer vacation had arrived, sending the children into a frenzy of nearly frantic fun-filled days. But after two weeks of glorious freedom... they were bored.

"There's nothing to do," they wailed.

I had an idea! "How about a neighborhood badminton tournament?"

So off they went to organize the event. After much discussion, two teams of four were formed, and two captains were carefully chosen.

My son Steven led the "Hawks," and Arnie Dick, the "Sidewinders."

The children who did not participate in the contest set up a refreshment stand and sold lemonade and cookies. They also stood on the sidelines and cheered for their favorite team... which changed according to the score.

A trophy was needed so I donated my green ceramic teapot, a gift from my niece Vicky.

At last, the games began!

Oh, it was a glorious match! The teams played six sets but the score tied, so two more sets were played. Then the score was four and four! They played two more sets and the "Sidewinders" won by one point!

As captain Arnie claimed the trophy... I realized that the dear old pot was gone forever.

Suddenly, Steven turned to Arnie and challenged him again. Once more the trophy was put on proud display, and once again the captains faced each other under the net.

After so many sets, the players were exhausted but the shuttle-cock remained in play and made countless trips between the courts.

It was another close match but in the end the "Hawks" were in possession of the trophy. Captain Steven placed it in my hands with a happy grin and a quick wink.

The old pot is retired now. It sits on a high shelf where it oversees the kitchen. Sometimes... when the night is full of cricket songs... the bright Ukrainian teapot recalls how it was lost, then saved, because a young boy knew his mother could not bear to see it taken.

PAMELA

I DON'T KNOW where she came from, but suddenly she arrived in the fourth grade at Madison Elementary School.

Somehow we chose each other and became friends.

An odd couple, I'm sure. For she was gifted with beauty: a halo of soft curls and a perfect little nose graced with nine discreetly golden freckles.

Pamela was good at everything she did and was the undisputed master of the parallel bars. Crowds gathered to watch her recess performance, and the fragrance of her laurels wafted about us as we walked arm in arm.

But her greatest talent was the ability to read so fast that all her words ran together in a wonderful lilt of exquisitely incomprehensible gibberish. Oh, how I longed to be so skilled!

During summer vacation I read thousands of pages aloud. Gaining momentum, I accelerated to a reckless pitch. Then... our family moved to another school district.

Now in the fifth grade of the new school, I enjoyed one breathless moment of glory which I dedicated to Pamela. I rapidly read my way through one lengthy paragraph of American geography before the amazed teacher rapped her ruler on her desk, peered at me over her spectacles, and said, "That will be enough."

And... it was.

TRUCKIN' WITH DAD

MY DAD, Gabriel George "Guy" LaDuke, had an old truck with a well-weathered wood flatbed. Sometimes he'd get a job hauling cargo, and if it was a big job, he needed a "navigator."

One day, he got a job hauling landscaping stones and required the assistance of his best navigator... me.

We laid a course for a rock quarry near Winona, Minnesota, and went out upon a memory-making adventure.

Dad didn't want to be late, so the ride down was a straight shot. We picked up some bologna, bread, and beer (Dad's Old-Fashioned Root Beer) and I slapped sandwiches together as we bounced merrily along.

Dad never said "make a sandwich." He'd say "Slap them together, Cracker Jack!" These particular sandwiches proved to be the best Dad had ever eaten, and he'd eaten "more than 6,000!"

Later, we sang loud, long songs and made elegant toasts to one another. The toasts were invariably followed by a reckless clash of pop bottles, manly swigs of root beer, and fits of laughter.

Eventually, we chugged up to a large metal shed and rolled an abrupt stop. We got out of the dusty cab and entered the dimly-lit stonemill.

I checked out the manner in which the rock slabs were ground, while Dad discovered that our stones were not quite ready. How long? A couple of hours!

Hooray! A couple of hours of unscheduled adventure! We plunged into the truck. Dad turned the key, punched the starter, and grinned as the engine roared to life.

We drove around town. It was clean and quiet. Great leafy trees canopied the sleepy streets.

Most memorable was our climb up a steep road which promised a grand view of the Mississippi River.

"We have to see it," Dad decided. "We might not come here again."

Oh, how the old truck chattered and fumed! Oh, how nervously I looked out the back window!

"Dad," I shouted, "we can't do it! We'll never make it!"

But Dad was deaf to my fearful screams. He simply laid his hand on the floor shift, depressed the clutch, and searched for a more adequate gear.

The truck lurched up the hill and at last, we gained the summit. Such a triumph required another root-beer toast. I toasted Dad. Dad toasted the truck.

Yes, it was worth the trip, because I'll never forget how Dad and I and the trusty truck made it to the top of Sugar Loaf Mountain.

THE SKIRT

WHEN I WAS SEVEN years old, my Aunt Gerry was the most wonderful person in my world. I used to enjoy watching her fix her hair, put on her make-up, and select items from her collection of costume jewelry to complement her clothing.

She was dressed like a princess one evening, and sat waiting for her friends. Her black hair was faultlessly curled, and her happy face flawless. She wore a crisp white blouse with puffed sleeves and a black taffeta skirt embellished with a red floral brocade.

"Aunt Gerry," I whispered, "can I have your skirt when you don't want it anymore?"

She leaned down and promised into my eager ear, "I'll save it for you."

For several days, I pretended that I was wearing the skirt as I danced through my grandmother's house on Franklin Avenue in Minneapolis. I could hear the taffeta rustle around me, and the coolness of the fabric brushed my ankles as I twirled and spun the days away.

Then I forgot all about my childish request. But my aunt did not.

When I was sixteen, a parcel arrived from St. Paul. Under layers of white tissue-paper, I discovered the black skirt.

I put it on... it was too big. So my mother cut and pinned and sewed and pressed the night away, and in the morning I put it on again and went to school.

Of course, I was too grown-up to spin and twirl... but the skirt rustled nicely as I swished down the corridors and up the stairs of the Cass Lake High School.

It was Mother's skill in sewing that rescued the old-fashioned skirt, and it was quilting that rescued a friend from a life of struggle and despair.

STAR QUILT

IT WAS, she said, a quilt that saved her life. It seems she'd lost her way, struggling over old traditions in conflict with new models. But during a period of great distress, she'd heard Grandmother's counsel, like a faint bell across a troubled sea. "Keep your hands busy," she'd called as from a memory.

It was so simple... so profound. So gentle... so powerful.

It was a storm of life that brought her to a peaceful shore... wrapped in a morning-star quilt.

Her life, though never free of struggle, became an ever-hopeful journey. However adverse the winds, no more would she be driven to the long, lonely shores of absolute despair.

Her hope renewed, her spirit reborn, her vision clear... she turned to the star for guidance. Like any good compass, it pointed the right way, but the course was hers to choose.

Oh, what a world of choice lay unexplored before her! Now, she'd found a medium to carry her message of hope to others... the message she'd discovered waiting in the folds of her first quilt.

With blessing and dignity, she began to cut and piece and sew until each star was completed. Then, another was begun... and so it went for many years.

Countless stars. Each so new and yet so old, so

similar and yet so diverse... so contrived and yet so unrestrained.

Pastels were arranged to carry the beholder on a journey across misty meadows and distant hills. Blues upon blues... like waves and tides of oceans visited in fancy. Bright golds exploded... like new-born suns on the edge of heaven. Vibrant jewel-tones... like sunlit cathedral windows calling her to prayer.

She saw it there in every quilt. That sweet, abundant hope that made life a gift too wonderful to waste.

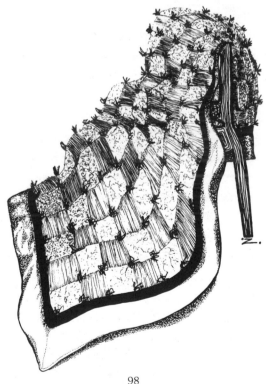

SHATTERED TRUST

WHEN I WAS still quite young, my father had a small truck market where he sold produce.

One day, he came to my Aunt Gerry's home in St. Paul and took me to work with him. The produce stand was located somewhere around Lake Calhoun in Minneapolis. Aunt Gerry didn't want me to go, but I begged her until she gave up in disgust and said, "Alright. But if anything should happen, call me. I'll come and get you."

"What could possibly go wrong?" I wondered as I hurried away with my dad.

It was always fun to go with him. He liked to try everything. Nothing seemed to frighten him. He did not worry about practical things. Some people thought he was a bit reckless... but he said he was "living for the moment."

It was sunny and nicely warm, so a lot of people stopped to look at our produce. Some of them bought a little... some of them bought a bunch.

It was mid-afternoon when Dad said, "I'll have to get some change. You keep the store open. When I get back, we'll work a couple of more hours and then I'll take you out for supper," he promised.

But he did not return. Still, ever hopeful, I kept watching and waiting. At last I took some coins and went out to find a pay phone.

I called Aunt Gerry. "Dad left me out here," I told her.

She was furious. "I'm coming right now. Lock yourself in and don't open the door until I get there."

I returned to "the store," as Dad called the little roadside stand, and started putting the produce inside. The night had grown chilly, the mosquitoes were hungry, and I was alone with my shattered trust and broken heart.

When my Aunt Gerry and Uncle Juel arrived, she scolded me for being concerned about the produce. "Let it rot," she seethed.

"It's his living," I countered.

Then I put the money in the metal box and hid it under the counter where Dad could find it when he came back to work.

Again she scolded me. "Take that money! You're the one who earned it. He already took his share."

So I took a few bills to satisfy her.

It was a quiet ride back to the house. I tried to act as though it didn't bother me, but Aunt Gerry knew how deeply I'd been hurt.

"You know what happened, don't you?" she asked.

"Yes," I answered.

He'd taken the money to buy a bottle, and his prosperity got the best of him. With money in his pocket... he'd found friends.

I could hear him making his old excuses. "I just couldn't leave while I still had money. The boys would do the same for me. Well, you're a big girl now. I figured you could take care of yourself... and you did just fine, too."

The truth was hard to take. He'd simply forgotten all about me... waiting alone in the cold night.

But I knew he'd wake up sick and sorry. He'd be ashamed, too.

"I won't hear from him again," I told my aunt, "not for a long, long time."

"That's right," she returned, "and don't you feel sorry for him, either."

But I did... and I do... and I always will.

NOT LONG AGO my young grandson, Royal, took possession of a small U.S. flag printed on plastic.

He immediately tacked it upside-down near the back door of his home on Tract 33, Cass Lake, Minnesota.

When an older visitor belittled him for putting it up wrong, Royal said, "This is a distress signal."

I wondered if the flag was a symbol of his personal distress... or the distress he has seen in his community, his school, and the Leech Lake Reservation.

Several days later, when I returned to visit the family, I discovered that the flag was upright.

Does this mean that the distress he saw around him no longer existed? Or does it mean that a small boy had been "silenced"? Was his conduct corrected to conform with that of the "good citizen"?

Perhaps the upright flag, for him, has become his signal that the sea of controversy is too terrible for a child to navigate alone.

NEVER ALONE AGAIN

H
E WALKED ALONE, carrying a small backpack. His long white hair fell over his face as he bent down to pick up a piece of rusted iron. He stood up slowly and tossed the metal into a growing heap near the railroad tracks.

I was walking the tracks, too. So I followed along behind him. I bent over, picked up a piece of iron, and tossed it into the pile he was building. He glanced at me briefly and continued his task.

We worked together for several minutes, and he never looked at me again.

So... I stepped closer and extended my hand. "Hello," I said. "My name is Anne."

After a long and deliberate period of consideration... he took my hand. His skin felt like paper, but his grasp was firm.

"My name is Harold," he returned.

"Do you live around here?" I asked.

His arm made a wide arc that seemed to take in all of north Grand Forks, North Dakota, as he replied, "Over there."

I stuck my cold hands into my jacket pockets as I continued, "Have you lived here long?"

"All my life," he said.

"Why are you picking up iron? Do you sell it?" I wanted to know.

"No," he answered, "I just put it into piles."

"Do you think I ask too many questions?"

He smiled broadly, "No. I do think you ask many questions... but not too many."

"Is it alright?" I asked.

"Of course," he replied. But his broad smile disappeared and a light blinked out behind his eyes as he added, "People usually aren't interested in an old man like me."

But I was interested. "Are you retired?"

"Yes, I used to build furniture. The Nordby building was a furniture manufacturing company. I worked there for fifteen years."

He stopped walking again and looked at me closely.

I wanted to hear more. "Well, I bet you've seen many changes in this town."

"Oh," he exclaimed with another wide wave of his arm, "the whole skyline has changed!"

"I went to the theater once," he continued. "It was quite elegant. A famous singer performed on the stage. Oh, she was beautiful!" Then the excitement drained from his voice. "No one like that comes here anymore."

"Do you have a family?" I asked.

"No," he answered.

"Do you live alone?"

"No," he said, as his eyes lit up and the broad smile returned. "I have a friend. Her name is Sally. Would you like to meet her?"

Without waiting for an answer, he pulled a tiny

afghan bundle out of his backpack. Carefully he unrolled it. Proudly he held the contents up for me to admire. Sally was a doll!

His smile never wavered. "Sally has her winter wardrobe on now. She has clothes for every season. When it gets too cold for her to go out with me, I set her in her chair and she waits for me. When I get home, she's always glad to see me."

He paused for a moment then added, "I used to be alone. But now I have Sally."

I watched him wrap Sally in her afghan and tuck her tenderly into the backpack.

He arranged her so that she could see us as we talked.

Finally he said, "I have to go home now." Reaching for my hand he added, "I'm so glad to meet you, Anne."

As we held hands, I looked into his pale, peaceful eyes.

"Goodbye, Harold," I said. With my other hand, I touched Sally's golden curls. "Goodbye, Sally," I whispered.

My hand slipped out of his and I turned to walk away.

When I got to the street, I looked back to see how far he had gone. He was standing in the same place! As I watched, a thin arm raised and a fragile hand waved to me.

I returned the wave as vigorously as possible.

I think I saw Sally's tiny hand wave, too.

I was working at the Grand Forks Herald then and lived alone in an apartment in the Dakota Block on Fourth Street.

Harold's wisdom made sense to me....

So... I went out one day and purchased a small stuffed bear. I called him Baby Blackfoot. When I went to work, I left him facing the door so we would see each other as soon as I came home.

I still have that little bear... and I still have the memory of a man named Harold and his special friend, Sally, who rescued him from loneliness and saved him from despair.

DAISY BLESSINGS

THE DAISIES along our road reach their peak in mid-June. That seems to signal to the county's grass-cutters that they must go forth immediately to destroy these roadside beauties.

With this in mind, I hastily harvested a generous supply to enjoy inside the house for several days. Those left behind were mowed down to lie gasping and writhing as they withered away.

However, several metal posts near our gravel drive keep even the most dedicated cutters at bay, and so I have a stand of white daisies guarding my road while the reliable brown-eyed Susans mature.

But today, something inside of me longs for a big bouquet of fresh daisies to grace the small, round table on the deck beside the yellow glider. So, accompanied by my good Lady and a persistent entourage of uninvited biting flies, I walk to a nearby field still hosting great drifts of the coveted blossoms.

The biting flies abandon us as we walk among the thigh-high flowers. Quietly and leisurely, I pick an armful while Lady dozes nearby. Then I hurry home where a container of cold water waits on the picnic table, ready to receive the "little priests"... as friend Aina calls them.

According to Aina, daisies look like fair-haired men in ruffled clergy collars, found gracing forgotten cemeteries and convent gardens.

Quickly I strip the lower leaves, snip off the long stems, and carefully arrange them in Aunt Audrey's old glass vase.

The vase has seen many more flowers since it came to be with me. My aunt admired the form and sparkle of the empty vase, while I enjoy it most when brimming with daisies.

Now... for a few more days... they will greet me as I leave or enter by the front door. And when they are old and tired, I will deposit them with ceremony beside the back door where they will decompose and nourish other nations that will rise up to bless me... next June!

CASKET PRACTICE THWARTED _____

WHEN I WAS NINE years old, it occurred to me that I should begin to practice how I would lie in a casket. It seemed a wise investment of time as I felt that I would die young.

Casket practice commenced on a humid afternoon in August. I lay with my hands carefully crossed over my thin chest and closed my eyes... just so. I allowed myself slow, shallow breaths and concentrated on... stillness.

Presently, I heard my sister sneak up and felt her breathing in my face. She smelled like scrambled eggs and catsup. She whispered my name and shook my shoulder.

"Stillness," I thought.

She pinched my arm terribly. "Stillness."

Suddenly she gasped and ran from the room screaming, "Mama, she's dead! She's real dead!"

The fingers of my left hand wandered to the terrible pinch, trying to comfort the burning flesh and rub away the pain.

I recrossed my arms as Mama's patient steps carried her to the bed. She sat down beside me and made strange choking sounds, as her body shook with what I imagined to be the passion of her grief upon discovering my dead body.

I opened my eyes to comfort her. "Mama," I whispered, "I'm not dead."

"I know that," she said, bursting into laughter. "But what are you doing?"

"I'm practicing how to lie in a casket," I answered sadly.

"Well," she said brightly. "Come with me. I think you should practice how to wash dishes."

SIR WALTER OF THE MOONLIGHT_____

IT WAS A WARM NIGHT and I had left the windows open to cool the house. So, out of the night, the sound came in through the open window.

"Chirrrp... chirrrp... chirrrp."

Six-year-old Wallis had been awakened by the strange sound and now she couldn't sleep.

"Chirrrp... chirrrp... chirrrp."

There it was again! Tingles of icy fear tip-toed up and down her spine.

"Chirrrp... chirrrp... chirrrp."

The strange sound reached out to her through the darkness. Cautiously, she uncovered one eye. She looked around the room, carefully inspecting each shadow. Then she uncovered the other eye. She saw nothing to fear.

Slowly she pushed back the blanket and dangled one thin leg over the side of the bed. All remained quiet. In one swift movement she sat up and swung both legs over the side of the bed. But she was too frightened to put her feet on the floor.

"Mommy," she wailed into the darkness beyond the bedroom door.

But Mommy did not answer. Wallis felt alone in the night-filled house.

Suddenly the strange sound reached out again.

"Chirrrp... chirrrp... chirrrp."

It pushed Wallis out of her safe bed and sent her running through the darkness. With a great leap, she flew over her father and landed in the cozy nest between her sleeping parents.

Father grunted noisily, turned heavily, and resumed his measured snore.

I raised my tired head and blinked my sleepy eyes. "What's going on?" I mumbled.

Wallis took my hand and pressed it over her galloping heart. I sat up. "What's wrong?" I asked.

"Mommy, I'm scared... something woke me up... something scary... I can't sleep."

"Well," I said with a touch of excitement. "This sounds like a midnight mystery. Come on. Let's go and find out about something scary."

Hand-in-hand, we stole across the moonlit living room.

Wallis noticed that the darkness seemed more friendly now.

When we reached the girls' room, I moved Annie closer to the wall and Wallis crawled in beside her. Then I lay down on the outside edge of the crowded bed.

"Chirrrp... chirrrp... chirrrp."

Wallis moved closer to me and slipped her thin arms around my neck. I held her small hands in mine. When she felt quite safe she asked, "What is that?"

"It's a little black field-cricket," I told her.

Wallis had seen crickets during the day. "A cricket is like a grasshopper," she recalled.

"But much finer," I said. "With his long thin legs, he's a bit of a dandy. And he's quite shy, you know."

Wallis agreed. She'd seen crickets scurry into dark hiding places when she tried to look at them too closely.

"But what a friendly gentleman he is," I continued. "And how dashing with his black polished armor, long black stockings, black suede boots, and sweeping black antennae."

"Does he have a name?" Wallis wanted to know.

"You can give him a name," I returned.

"Do you think he'd like to be called Walter?" Then remembering the polished armor, long stockings, suede boots, and sweeping antennae, Wallis added, "Sir Walter... Sir Walter of the Moonlight."

I smiled.

"Chirrrp... chirrrp... chirrrp."

"How does he make that sound?" she wondered without alarm.

"He rubs the hard edges of his wings together," I said. "I think it's a bit like playing a violin."

"Chirrrp... chirrrp... chirrrp," Sir Walter played, adding his fine music to the night.

Wallis smiled, closed her eyes, and drifted off to sleep. Sir Walter's large friendly face came into her dream. She smiled at him as he bowed deeply, his long antennae sweeping down to rest briefly on her cheek.

I had slipped out of bed and kissed Wallis on the cheek, then walked through the quiet house to my room.

But as I stepped into the living room... I raised up on my toes, stretched my arms high above my head, and danced in the moonlight spilling through the large front window.

As I danced, Sir Walter raised his silver bow and, touching the strings of his golden violin, he played a midnight concert.

"Chirrrp... chirrrp... chirrrp... chirrrp... chirrrp."

Finally I curtsied, my hair falling over my face... and somewhere in the darkness beyond my window, Sir Walter of the Moonlight laid aside his instrument and bowed deeply.

The moon still calls me to dance... and sometimes to witness the moon-dances of other nations.

CORN DANCE

I VISITED MY GARDEN one night hoping to alarm the raccoons who had been feasting on my corn.

I stalked along the perimeter, leaving my footprints reeking with human odor.

This done, I stood in the moonlight to contemplate the corn and thank Great Spirit for another good harvest. Traditionally, Ojibwe women raise the family food. Once again, I was part of the great cycle of life.

My contemplative spirit and the mystery of moonlight took charge of the moment, and the tall corn plants were transformed. They became people. Holding the corn at their sides, they stood poised for dance.

In the shadows of the trees, the broad shiny corn leaves became great feathered bustles. The upright tassels became proud roaches, the feathered head-dresses of ceremonial dancers.

Then a gentle breeze made its way up from the foggy river, bringing life to the dancers.

The great feathers swayed and shook, the proud roaches bobbed and bounced... and the corn danced in the moonlight.

THE FIRST BLUEBIRD _____

IT HAPPENED in the long ago that a small, drab bird longed to be bright and beautiful.

One night, the bird dreamed that Great Spirit spoke to him. "Go to Magic Lake. Bathe in the water three times a day. Do this for seven days. In the end, you will become more beautiful than you could ever imagine."

When the bird awoke, he flew quickly to Magic Lake and bathed. On the sixth day, the little bird wondered what form his beauty would take. He imagined himself with a great green tail and a silver crest upon his yellow head.

But when he stepped out of the water that day, all his feathers fell off! He was naked!

"I'm so ashamed!" he cried. "I don't want to be beautiful. I don't care to have a green tail and a silver crest. I want my old feathers back."

He hid in the tall grass and fell asleep. He dreamed that a small blue spirit-bird found him. He looked at the blue bird and thought, "How pretty she is. If I could look like her, I wouldn't want anything else."

In the morning, he bathed again and saw that his feathers were already growing back. When he bathed a third and last time... all his feathers burst out! They were as blue as the sky!

Then he heard a sweet song and looking up, he saw

the little blue spirit-bird sitting on a low branch just above him. He flew up and sat with her.

Soon, they built a nest and she laid three blue eggs. It wasn't long before the first little bluebirds broke out of their eggs. It wasn't much longer before they were able to fly.

They learned to sing their mother's sweet song and like their father, they carried the sky on their backs.

As we consider the origins of the first bluebird, so must we consider the possibility that, unless we do what we can to protect other nations and the earth... our Mother... we may someday see the last bluebird.

MOTHER MOUNTAIN

I HAVE STRUGGLED breathlessly to this strong peak and have been greeted by a grand Black Hills panorama. On every side there are ancient ones... Grandfathers.

I arrive... a stranger encouraged by the songs of western birds. Far below, the river sends a gentle voice to me.

Aina and Marissa, my friends, were sleeping when I left my tent for a solitary adventure.

The air is thinner than in the woodlands of Minnesota and forces me to rest often. My physical limitations urge me to be cautious, and my feet seek secure stepping places.

On the east, the sun feels quite warm, but the cool air lifts my hair and reminds me of how cold the night was.

The black, jagged rock drops suddenly away, and my stomach rises to my throat. I see a bit of river sparkle up at me.

In this high place, the mullein candelabra stand. Soon the golden flowers will burst into bloom, lighting their tall tapers and sending their glow into dark nights.

Great straight pines, rooted far below, send their green spires higher still. Many twisted trees are also here... stunted perhaps by the harshness that comes with winter. The tree tops look like the driftwood that

Minnesota's lakes toss upon sandy shores.

The lichens have been painting here. Their ageless patterns have charm that will escape the quick blink of my little camera.

There is not as much hairy moss hanging from these trees as from the trees that guard our quiet little camp.

The Black Hills rise around me and the wind speaks eloquently of all the things that really matter... here, in this place of the heart of everything that is.

FALL

FALL

HOW TURTLE CRACKED HIS SHELL _____

IT HAPPENED ONE DAY in the long ago, as the aspen leaves were falling all around and the birds were preparing to fly south, that Turtle asked, "Why do you go away? Why can't you stay here with me?"

"Soon the winter spirits will return to this land," said Robin.

"They bring cold and snow," said Bluebird.

"We won't be able to find food then," said Hummingbird.

"In the south it is always warm," sang Bluebird.

"With plenty of food," hummed Hummingbird.

Turtle, who was always interested in good food, said, "I want to go, too."

"Can you fly?" laughed Robin.

"Of course not," snapped Turtle.

"Well, it's a long walk," Bluebird twittered.

"Surely you can help me," begged Turtle. "If you wanted to take me with you... you would find a way!"

The birds talked it over.

Then Robin asked, "Can you hold a stick in your mouth?"

"I certainly can," boasted Turtle. "When I get something in my mouth, I never let it go."

Then Robin asked Blackbird and Crow if they would carry Turtle on a stick so he could go south with them.

"Very well," they replied.

So Turtle picked up the stick with his mouth. Blackbird and Crow took the ends in their claws and carried Turtle up into the sky.

Oh, it was so exciting! Turtle had never seen so many wonderful things before. He wanted to know everything. He wanted to know where they were. He wanted to know how far they had traveled. He wanted to know when they would arrive in the south.

Finally, he opened his mouth to ask his questions and... he fell off the stick! He tumbled end over end, all the way down to the earth.

When he hit the ground, his smooth polished shell cracked but it didn't break off. He looked up but the birds were too far away to call. Then he felt his shell shifting in a loose and terrible manner, and he suddenly lost interest in going south.

Turtle was glad to be alive, but he felt a little sick. So he found a small lake and swam to the bottom where he buried himself in the mud and went to sleep.

Today, Turtle still sleeps through the winter and carries a cracked shell.

The Lakota people often point to Turtle and tell their children to learn from his example.

They tell their children, "Sometimes it is best if you keep your mouth shut."

ONLY THE OLD ONES speak of how the people suffered during the hungry-time.

It occurred in late winter or early spring... when snow covered the ground and the supply of stored food dwindled.

This was a time of starving for many.

It was a time when babies cried desperately for food. Mothers wept in despair, and fathers turned their backs to hide their tears. It was a time when grandmothers crooned of their grief, and grandfathers remembered all the years of hungry-times.

But the old ones also say that Great Spirit saw how the people suffered and pitied them. So Great Spirit blessed the people with a gift of *mahnomen* (wild rice), the food that grows on water.

Soon the people found rice growing in many shallow lakes and rivers. Not only was rice provided, but with it came the knowledge to preserve this food through the entire circle of seasons. So the hungry-time was nearly eliminated.

There are several versions of how this occurred but I like to think that the knowledge came through holy dreams that blessed the sleep of certain people.

SHEE-SHEEB BRINGS A MESSAGE _____

AS THE OJIBWE people were pushed westward, they followed the waterways by canoe into the Great Lakes country, where they settled. The women set up camp, and the men went out to hunt.

One of the young men sat alone by a quiet river, wondering what would happen to his people in the strange new place. Soon he became weary and fell asleep.

As he slept, Shee-sheeb (duck) came to him in a dream and said, "It is time for you to learn about Mahnomen." Then Shee-sheeb told this story:

"In the long ago, Mahnomen was a good and wise man. I was his messenger and spent much time with him.

"At first, Mahnomen cared only about the welfare of his people, so the band flourished and became many. But as he grew older... he grew selfish as well. Then he withheld his wisdom. He asked for material things in exchange for knowledge. Soon he was a rich man, but he'd lost favor with his tribe and the good spirits that bring good things.

"While Mahnomen prospered, his people became increasingly despondent and soon they changed many of their good ways. They became lazy and did not care that their children suffered many hardships.

"Great Spirit looked down upon the pitiful people

and grieved. Now he must punish the proud Mahnomen.

"One day Mahnomen went out on the lake to get some fish for his supper. Suddenly a strong wind began to blow, raising the water into high waves. His canoe was tossed up and then dashed against the stones in the bottom of the lake. The boat split, the cedar ribs snapped, and the bark was shredded into tiny pieces.

"Mahnomen was terrified and he knew he could not survive. He begged Great Spirit to forgive his selfishness and greed. He asked that his death would somehow bring great good to his people. He prayed for a blessing upon all the generations that would follow his.

"Mahnomen's body was never found. But from that day to this... wild rice has grown in the flowing rivers and shallow waters of the Great Lakes area."

These are the things Shee-sheeb told the sleeping man.

After the young man awoke, he was surprised to see Shee-sheeb eating strange-looking seeds that had fallen on a lily pad. The man walked into the water to examine them.

Once more Shee-sheeb spoke. "This is the good berry. This is the food Mahnomen left to sustain his people. This is the gift from Great Spirit. Take care of it. Tell your people that all generations must care for the wild rice. If they do not, it will be taken from them."

MANY ANISHINABE Ojibwe still remember the not-so-long-ago when a lake was flagged to signal the rice harvest.

The man in charge of flagging the lake usually lived nearby and knew the character of the lake and the nature of the rice it produced.

It was his duty to watch the rice through its growing season and determine when it was ready for harvest. When the rice was fully mature, he raised a white flag on a tall pole which could be seen all around the lake.

When the people saw it, they went into the rice beds and the annual harvest was begun.

To avoid depleting the rice bed and to prolong a good harvest, the head man might lower the flag for a few days after opening the bed. This gave the later rice a chance to ripen.

Several years ago, I asked some old-timers if the flag was ever violated. None of them recalled that anyone ever ignored the council of the head man.

They said the people respected his decision and left the rice bed when the flag was lowered.

Everyone understood that the duty of the head man was to protect the rice. In protecting this, he was preserving a good life for all the people.

When we were children, the elders warned us that the day was coming when their council would no longer be respected. They told us that the gift of *mahnomen* would be taken from us.

We see this happening now.

Too many people have forgotten to be thankful, to put back rice seed, and to share with those who are physically unable to harvest their own.

Today the precious and endangered natural wild-rice beds are viewed by many as nothing more than an opportunity for exploitation.

The consequences of such conduct is certain.

As the wise ones have said, "What we do to Turtle Island, we do to ourselves."

THE CORNHUSK DOLL _____

IT HAPPENED in the long ago that Great Spirit created the three sisters to sustain the life of the two-leggeds. The three sisters are beans, corn, and squash.

Now, Corn Sister wanted to do more for the people. She wanted to give a gift to the children so two-leggeds would always love her.

Great Spirit was pleased with the generosity of the corn sister and granted her a special blessing. He took her husks and formed a doll. He made the cornhusk doll tall and graceful and beautiful.

The cornhusk doll traveled from village to village and everywhere she went, she was told how beautiful she was... and soon she began to think so, too.

It wasn't long before she had become conceited and arrogant. She would often sit beside a still pool and admire her reflection all day. "Yes," she would tell herself, "I really am quite beautiful."

One day Great Spirit called her. He said she should remember that Corn Sister wanted her to be a blessing to the two-legged children. He warned Cornhusk Doll that if she did not overcome her conceit, she would have to be punished.

At first Cornhusk Doll tried to be gracious and humble, but everyone persisted in telling her of her beauty. In time, she forgot Great Spirit's warning.

One day she was sitting by the pool, looking at her

reflection and thinking how dreadful it would be if she had not been created beautiful. Suddenly she was unable to see. She covered her face with her hands. She could not feel her eyes! She could not feel her mouth! Her nose and ears had also disappeared!

She could not even weep! Suddenly her feet seemed to come out from under her and she fell to the ground. She realized that now she was no bigger than a rabbit.

Later that day, a little child found her lying helpless in the grass and carried her home. The child loved the no-face doll and soon other children wanted no-face cornhusk dolls, too. Mothers learned to make such dolls and from that day, every generation of children has enjoyed them.

So Corn Sister has had her wish.

But the no-face doll is also a reminder that we should not think beauty makes us superior to others. The no-face doll warns us that we must guard ourselves from becoming conceited, self-centered, and arrogant.

THE BUFFALO WOMAN _____

THE WESTERN ANISHINABE tell the story of a young woman who was greatly honored because she listened carefully to instructions and did as she was told.

It happened long ago that the buffalo had left the country, and a time of famine had come upon the people.

Three sisters who had married the same man were out gathering firewood. The youngest one was carrying the heaviest load, and her leather carrying-strap broke.

Her sisters helped her repair the strap and retie her bundle of wood. But she had not gone far when it broke again. This time they waited as she mended her strap and tied up her wood, then they went on together.

Once more the strap broke, and the wood tumbled to the ground. This time the two older women returned to their lodge and left their sister to resolve her problems.

When the young woman was alone, she heard a small voice singing. The voice seemed to be quite near. She looked around but saw no one. She was frightened and wanted to run away, but she didn't know which way to run.

"Don't be afraid," the voice said. "I will not harm you."

"Where are you?" the woman asked.

"Here, by the wood," the voice answered.

Then the woman noticed an unusual stone lying on

the ground near her scattered wood.

"Woman," the stone said, "take me to your camp."

The woman tucked the stone under her belt, picked up her wood, and went home. She did not tell anyone what had happened.

One night, in a dream, the stone spoke to her. "I came to your people because they are poor and hungry. So I pity them. I came to you because you are humble and I know that all your thoughts are good."

The stone told her what she must do to help her people.

"Ask your husband to invite the good men of the village to your lodge tomorrow night. I will teach you songs and a ceremony which you must show them.

"If you do this, the buffalo will return. But you must warn the people that my power will come like a great wind and arrive as a lone bull. Tell your people not to harm the bull, but to let him pass safely through the camp. Soon a herd will follow.

"You must be certain that no harm comes to the first buffalo or, hungry as you are, there will be no more buffalo and your people will starve."

During the dream she learned many songs. When she awoke, she wondered how she should speak to her husband.

Being the youngest wife, she was the one who slept near the door of the lodge. She was the one least honored.

Only the first wife who sat beside their husband

could take part in such an important ceremony. So the young woman decided that she must tell the first wife everything. The older woman was shocked at what she heard, but she knew her sister wouldn't lie. So she agreed to speak to their husband about the matter.

When their husband was informed of all these things, he immediately sent word to the good men of the village.

When they gathered in the home of the young woman, she served dried berries and meat. When they had eaten, the husband told them why they had been called together.

Some of the men were excited about the woman's dream. Others were disgusted and refused to believe that a woman had been granted such a holy vision. These men left in anger and would not participate in the ceremony.

With the approval of the remaining men, the husband asked his youngest wife to sit at the head of the lodge and lead the ceremony that had been shown to her in the dream.

The woman prayed a long prayer, and then she

began to sing one of the songs she had heard in the dream. During the ceremony, she passed the stone to her husband and he was able to sing the song, too. So the stone was passed to each man and they were able to sing the songs with the woman and her husband.

When the singing was finished, she told them of the warning in her dream. So a crier was sent throughout the camp telling the people to prepare for a great storm.

"Tie down your lodges and all your possessions or you will lose everything," they warned. "Do not harm the bull that will walk through the village."

Some of the people laughed and said it was foolish to believe the dreams of such a young woman. But others carefully followed her instructions, although there was no sign of a storm.

Long after dark, the weather began to change. A breeze began to move the treetops. Before long, it became a strong wind which shook the lodges.

Suddenly all the people were awakened by the loud cracking sound of a great cottonwood tree being blown over.

The lodges that had not been secured were blown away. Those who had scoffed at the young woman saw their possessions scattered by the mighty wind. How frightened they were as they ran to seek shelter among the lodges that were standing firm in the terrible storm!

While the people prayed for safety, they heard the loud hoofbeats and heavy breathing of a lone bull wandering through the camp.

No one dared to harm him.

In the morning, the storm ceased suddenly and the people crept out of their lodges. They saw a large herd of buffalo grazing not far from the camp.

The men were able to bring down as many as they needed, for the animals were not alarmed.

The women wept with happiness at having real food again. Now they would have hides to replace their worn-out robes and patch the holes in their moccasins.

A thanksgiving feast was held, and everyone watched as the young wife was seated beside her husband. So she was honored all the days of her life and still the people tell her story.

Today, a white buffalo calf has come among us to remind us that we are brothers that need each other.

JOURNEY TO THE WHITE BUFFALO CALF

I HAD BEGUN my pilgrimage to the white buffalo calf almost as soon as I heard she'd been born. But other commitments kept me home, and several weeks passed before I was actually on the long, long road to Janesville, Wisconsin.

I would join friends and fellow peacemakers, Ann Mikkelsen and Roberto Rodriguez, in Minneapolis. Together we would journey to the 46-acre farm that had been chosen for the birth of the white buffalo calf of prophecy.

In preparation, I had cut a stack of cloth squares to make prayer-ties on the way. I didn't count them until after I was finished cutting. The number was 83, which is also the number of years between the Wounded Knee Massacre (1890) and the Wounded Knee Occupation (1973). Somehow, I feel that arriving at this number "by accident" is significant to my personal journey.

We arrived at the Dave and Valerie Heider farm on a cool but pleasant day. Dry leaves were blowing about in eager swirling dances, while waves of migrating birds and waterfowl passed overhead.

I completed the last prayer-tie as Roberto pulled the car into the second parking lot along the Rock River near the Heider farm. The gracious Caucasian elder man parking cars appealed to me greatly; I recognized in him a deep and sincere respect for persons of

Anishinabe heritage.

According to Floyd Hand, a spiritual leader from Pine Ridge, South Dakota, the calf will bring purity of mind, body, and spirit; she will also unify all nations. Others say she signals the beginning of a new era of reconciliation among the races and a greater respect for our Mother Earth.

Miracle, the calf who was a symbol of hope, rebirth, and unity, was born August 20, 1994 (my grandson Justice was born the following morning). I have been told that, because of wholesale slaughter of the buffalo nation during the last century, the chances of a white buffalo being born today is one in six billion.

Although Heider has received several offers, he refuses to sell the calf because he recognizes her significance.

The first thing I saw as I passed the barn and crested the hill approaching the buffalo enclosure was a gate, covered with gifts lifting and fluttering on the breeze. Synchronized by the wind, the movement was a living, breathing dance of welcome. It was a wonderful discovery and I stopped for several minutes to absorb the essence of it.

Some of the gifts left on and near the gate included feathers, sage, cedar, tobacco, prayer-ties, poems, letters, photographs, dream-catchers, baskets, beadwork, ribbons, corn, pumpkins, potatoes, squash... and the blue fabric braid we left there. I can still see it, nestled among the offerings... just a small object easily overlooked, but joined with all the others in a company of greatness.

Spiritual leader Arvol Looking Horse told Heider that, with the exception of eagle feathers, he can remove the items from the fence after four days and burn them. The smoke will carry them to the spirits. Surely our gift has been burned by now.

Encircled by the adult buffalo, the calf was sleeping midway up the hill behind the fence. Beyond the hill, to the left, was a tree or post with additional offerings waving in the breeze.

I wanted to isolate myself from the crowd at the fence but it was difficult. I finally joined my friends at the extreme right of the area designated for calf-watching and began to pray. I told the calf that I had come from Leech Lake, where many of my family and friends lived. I told her that our pitiful leaders were selling us out and destroying our future. I asked Great Spirit to bless them with wisdom and strength. Then I thanked Creator for sending the calf with this message of new hope for all nations.

I offered the prayer-ties and said that I would carry them back to Leech Lake to be blessed by a spiritual leader. I will also take them into a sweat. Afterwards they will be given to elders who cannot make the long journey to Janesville.

As I stood near the fence, a tall Anishinabe man in a faded denim jacket spoke to me. "Today you and I are doing something amazing," he said. "In all the world... this is the only place where such a creature lives... and we are here. Here we are standing in this place... at this time... looking at a miracle." His voice was hushed with the awesomeness of such a wonder.

Yes, I thought, whole nations have lived and died waiting for this calf.

While I considered the honor of being so privileged, Heider came out to feed the buffalo. Although it was clear that they shared an affectionate respect for the man who was their keeper... it seemed a bit incongruous that such great and powerful creatures would tag along after a man carrying a bucket of corn... romping and cavorting with childish glee in anticipation of the meal they would shortly enjoy.

When the calf advanced to the water trough near the gift laced gate, the crowd sighed in unison, and I imagined that our breaths were forever and unforgettably mingled in that place.

Before I left the gate area I looked for the tall man. I didn't know him and I'll probably never see him again... but I felt a healing experience in his presence and I wanted to shake his hand. When I found him, all I could say was, "Have a good journey." But... I think it was enough.

Heider has said that he will have the calf tested as soon as the protective 1,000-pound mother allows. The test will disclose whether she is a true white buffalo.

I observed that her new hair appears brown and her face is darker, too. But I am not dismayed.

I agree with the white elder man who told us as we

were leaving, "I don't care if she turns purple. She'll always be the white buffalo calf to me."

Then with tears glittering in his pale eyes, he reached into the car, and we held his thin hand. "May the Good Spirit be with you," he said.

Farther down the homeward road I recalled that man and considered his parting words. If I'd taken time to hear his story, perhaps he would have said, "I have been living here by the Rock River for many years. It's been a good life... and I'm not complaining. But the arrival of the white buffalo calf at my neighbor's farm has been an incredible event. It has opened my eyes... it has enhanced my understanding. Clearly I see that we are all related."

Perhaps he would have flung out his once-strong arms to include all of creation... the vital air, the nurturing nations of trees, the grandfather stones, and the life-giving water that has been flowing past his house for such a long, long time.

PEACE FLOAT

IT WAS A DAY well-chosen. Bright with sunlight, blessed with breeze. After selected music full of hope... we encouraged one another with good words.

Stories were presented... poems read.

Then, little glowing paper lanterns were set out upon the waters of Fishhook Lake. Slowly, satin-smooth ripples carried the small lights through the twilight.

One lantern, set out last, did not keep up. Some trick of the current kept it far behind. It dipped and twirled on the water... in no hurry to complete the course.

Then a curious beaver came out from the shoreline, swimming out beyond the dock. When satisfied no threat had been intended, he slid beneath the dark surface and disappeared.

Quietly canoes paddled out, gentle hands retrieved the lighted lanterns, and prayerful breaths put out each small fire.

The float event was an affirmation that peace-lovers around the world have joined hands, and in the joining of many hands there is strength.

LEAVING THE WOODS

I MUST LEAVE the woods to spend a few days in Minneapolis. When I return... the leaves will all have fallen.

Therefore, I ordered my day with time for a long, leisurely stroll through beauty, such as only autumn can provide.

Lady flushed a partridge. It didn't go far. Roosting in a small oak, it kept one anxious eye on the dog while the other was fixed on me.

Then on a pine-crowned hill I sat, with Lady patient by my side. From time to time, she raised her nose to smell whatever offering the wind had carried to us from some far place. A few crickets in the grass played their last songs.

The sky had spread the river with a rippled azure mantle. Raked by the wind, tawny grasses whispered tales I could no longer understand.

A variety of seeds imbedded themselves in my sleeves. Plucking them off, I sowed next year's wild-flowers.

Then I left the woods and stepped onto the narrow road to witness a delightful event. Hurrying toward me... each one with a sharp needle... they came, and I watched a thousand aspen leaves darning up the sandy road.

"No Trespassing," a sign suddenly shouted. But the

aspen leaves, like eager children, dashed across the guarded turf. A tall tangle of white clover tried to obscure the next sign. Looking up I wondered, "Do outlaw chickadees find shelter in those forbidden boughs?"

"No-tres-pass-ing," the wasted syllables marched off my tongue and fell down before me.

Farther on, the land became more friendly, and no sign ordered the nuthatch away. Hayfields mown not so long ago still sweeten the day. I stood so long, the Midas-sun was turning me to gold.

But a cold persistent wind pushed me homeward... although like a tardy child, my heels dragged just a little.

Near my road, I found two white daisies yawning in the sun. A few steps beyond were three brown-eyed Susans with plans to stay out late.

There is no gift like a lovely day.

MOM

She took me hunting,
Left me on the first stand
With a single-shot .22,
Signaled "quiet" thru pursed lips
Crossed with a gloved finger.
Stepping softly through
A kaleidoscope of fallen leaves
She disappeared...
Leaving me alone
Under a tall white birch.
Before dark she returned
To guide me home.

IT HAPPENED ONE DAY while I was on a good deer-stand that a brisk cold wind blew up. Within a few minutes, I had become quite chilled and decided to seek shelter. In a clearcut area, I climbed up on a brush pile and pulled out enough sticks so I could crawl down into the pile. I left the rifle above, pulled up my collar, and fell asleep.

When I awoke it was getting dark, so I thought I'd better find the road. I peeked up out of the brush pile and saw several deer feeding nearby. I watched them for a few minutes before I climbed out into the open. They raised their heads in unison to look at me. Then they returned to their evening meal. I guess they thought I was a bear.

Since it had grown too dark to hunt, I hung the rifle in the crook of my arm and walked back to the road.

As I walked along, I told myself a story.

A certain man went out in the fall to hunt a bear. It was very cold and had begun to snow. The hunter found a bear in a hole, killed it, and skinned it.

In the meantime, the cold wind had chilled the man through. So he decided to crawl into the hole to keep warm. He pulled leaves and grass over the opening and went to sleep.

When he woke up, he pushed the dried debris

away and looked out. What he saw surprised him greatly. Outside of the hole lay the rotten carcass of a bear, and it was covered with flies.

The man crawled out of the hole and found that it was spring.

He had slept all winter in the bear's den!

That is why the elders always say, "Never fall asleep in a bear's den."

They also say it is our brother Bear who sends the winter spirits of snow and cold back to the far north and invites the green spirits back to our land.

Many stories tell of the benevolence of Bear. Brother Bear is a cultural hero... ever ready to help the two-leggeds.

HE WANTED TO DIE _____

THE HEAD MAN of a certain band of a certain tribe of a certain nation had a foolish son who was disobedient and lazy. He was also a thief and rarely bathed. His father was ashamed of him, his sisters hated him, and his mother was heart-broken.

While the people busily prepared to move their camp, Lazy Boy slept. When they were ready to leave, the head man shook Lazy Boy to wake him.

"You're of no use to us," he told him. "You will remain here alone. I advise you to fast and pray for wisdom."

Lazy Boy watched the people cross the great lake in their birchbark canoes. Only his mother looked back, then lifted her arm to wave a last farewell.

It was autumn, the time of falling leaves.

Lazy Boy wanted to die, so he teased Black Bear to make him angry. He thought Bear would kill him, but Bear knew he was the abandoned son of a worthy man.

"He's pitiful," Bear thought. "I'll leave him alone."

Two times Bear tried to avoid the boy. The third time, Lazy Boy laid down in front of Bear and begged Bear to kill him.

But Bear slapped Lazy Boy in his fat belly and said, "Get up! Soon it will be winter. Because I pity you, I will take you to my den."

Bear gave Lazy Boy two blueberries for his hunger,

and each time he ate them, two more appeared.

During the whole winter, Lazy Boy listened to Bear's songs of courage and honor. At last Bear said, "Tomorrow we will leave the den. It is time for you to find your people."

The next day Bear pointed Lazy Boy in the right direction and sent him away. Lazy Boy traveled for two days. As he came near the village, he could smell the people. The odor made him so sick that he laid down and died.

Some children playing in the woods found the body. They ran to camp and told the leader.

An attempt was made by the medicine man to revive Lazy Boy, but it did no good.

At last Lazy Boy's weeping mother was allowed to build a small fire near his body. She covered the fire with sage, producing a heavy smoke which restored her son to life.

Lazy Boy was no longer fat, but well-formed and strong. He said that Bear had cared for him all winter. "He taught me many things," he told his father.

Lazy Boy had received counsel from Bear and it changed the way he thought. It changed his conduct as well. In time he became a wise leader and a respected head man. His people called him... Lone Bear.

LOST CHILD

IT HAPPENED in the long ago that a little girl went out to pick berries with her mother.

They came upon a small patch of the bright fruit and the eager child cried, "Berries! Here are berries! Let's pick them."

But her mother said, "We must find more berries. This is such a small patch. We'll go on farther."

They came to another small berry-patch and the child said, "I want to pick these berries." So she sat down and began to pick.

"Very well," the mother said, "you pick here and I will go on a little farther. You stay right here and wait for me. I'll come back for you." Then she left.

The little girl picked all the berries and then sat

down to wait. Soon it was dark, so she went to sleep.

In the morning, she ate her berries as she waited for her mother to return. As it grew dark again, the child became frightened and began to cry.

"Mama!" she screamed. But there was no answer. So she cried herself to sleep.

The next day she left the place and began to walk. In a short time she realized that she was lost. She sat down and cried again.

Suddenly she heard a woman call, "What's wrong, Little One? Why do you weep?"

She looked up to see a tall, handsome woman and two children coming toward her. The child was over-joyed to see them. She ran into the woman's out-stretched arms. They sat down together, and the woman held the child as the youngster told how she had become so lost.

The tall woman listened to the child's story and comforted her. Then she carried the young one to a nearby lake, bathed her, and afterwards gathered some sweet berries and good roots for the child to eat.

"Come, Little One," the woman said. "I'll take you to your people."

How happy the child was to hear that the woman knew where her people were. She wasn't lost anymore. She was going home!

Along the way, the other two children wanted to play, but the woman scolded them. "Little One does not want to play. She is feeling sad. Don't bother her."

The woman held the little girl's hand as they all walked along together.

When they got close to the village, the woman pointed out the direction the girl should go. Then she took her two children and went on her way.

"Good-bye," the girl called. The woman waved farewell.

The people in the village greeted the child with great joy, for she'd been missing several days. Her mother, however, had not returned.

When they asked the child how she'd found her way back, she told them about the tall woman and led them to the place they had parted.

The people were amazed to find the tracks of a large bear and two cubs.

So it was a female bear who had heard the child crying and taken pity. She and her cubs had appeared to the child as a woman with two children. This is one reason the Anishinabe Ojibwe often view Bear as a close relative.

THE RAG MAN

I WAS ALMOST SIX when the Rag Man entered my life. He came down Franklin Avenue pushing a creaking cart. I watched from the front bay window as he went by shouting, "Rags! Rags! Pennies for your rags."

Several days later, I heard him coming again and I flew to the window. Once more I watched him shuffle by behind the cart. I saw that his shoes were old, his coat was old... and his black hat had been worn for a long, long time.

"Grandma," I asked, "do we have any rags for the Rag Man?"

She rummaged through the closet and came out with two shirts... one was blue. "Here," she said in a soft voice, "you can give these to him."

I kept the shirts rolled up on the floor near the door and waited for him to come again.

At last I heard him shouting, "Rags! Rags! Pennies for your rags."

Quickly I gathered my proud bundle and ran out to wait for him.

I held up my rags as he stopped in front of our house. He examined them closely, and one by one he put them in the cart with the rest of his rags. Then he pressed two pennies into my waiting hand, leaned against the cart to get it rolling and went on, calling, "Rags! Rags! Pennies for your rags."

I sold a lot of rags that summer and I saved a lot of pennies.

I asked Grandma what the man did with so many rags.

"He sells them," she answered.

I also wondered where Grandma found so many rags for me to sell. But I didn't ask. I just went on doing my share to keep the Rag Man in business.

Suddenly he wasn't coming anymore.

"Where do you think he is?" I asked Grandma.

"He must be buying rags on another street," she told me.

"I think he must be sick," I worried.

I wondered if he was alone. I wanted to believe that someone would be there to hold his hand when he was afraid.

At last I told myself, "The Rag Man has died." I wept for several days and wanted to visit his grave. Grandma said that was quite impossible.

I've never forgotten him. I still think of him often.

Sometimes I close my eyes and on the wings of fancy I am carried back to Franklin Avenue. I see myself standing on the curb with my bundle of rags. I hear him first and then I see him.

Slowly he comes, pushing the creaking handcart. I hold the rags out to him and he takes them. Then he presses another penny into my hand. Once again he resumes his Franklin Avenue trade. "Rags! Rags!" he calls. "Pennies for your rags."

TO SWEEP A FLOOR _____

FLOOR SWEEPING is a job which can be accepted with enthusiasm by young children. The manner in which a child is instructed will not alter the style of sweeping that is eventually adopted. Instead, floor sweeping should be viewed as a demonstration of individuality. The craft should not be confined to the female gender, either.

I believe it is important to recognize the personality factor in order to avoid an overly critical attitude or any child-damaging comments.

Young children are eager to assume suitable responsibilities... for the reward of our approval. As the mother of six, I have been in the enviable position of observing several sweeping methods.

First, we have the "only-what-I-can-see" method. This child usually sweeps the middle of the room and other large exposed areas of the floor surface. This casual approach to floor sweeping can be annoying if we fail to realize that this child is not shirking duty when spaces under chairs are neglected. This child has many momentous thoughts tumbling through the mind during the floor-sweeping exercise. Astounding matters are being considered... matters more wonderfully important than a thousand well-swept floors.

The second is the thorough sweeper. This child pokes the business end of the broom into every corner, explores every obstacle that might hinder the dirt search. A reasonable degree of such concern can be gratifying, but consistent and extreme dedication to this non-vital activity is cause for alarm. Usually the child who adopts such a method is in need of special attention and personal approval, and will readily resort to less meticulous efforts when the inner person has been comforted and assured.

The third type is on a quest of discovery. The big-push sweeper discovers that the broom can also function somewhat like a shovel. The dirt is scooped up and tossed ahead with an abrupt motion. The child quickly steps forward and repeats the action. While the dust swirls, a second discovery is made. The broom may be entirely forgotten as the child examines a thousand dust motes shining in sunbeams gone astray. A close observation is made of the fine particles, reflecting light like a galaxy of little lazy worlds. Soon the wonder is exhausted, the broom is abandoned, and the child is gone... on to new discoveries.

The dancer is another impressive type... who must be observed from a concealed vantage point or the performance is not forthcoming. How tenderly the enchanted handle of the wooden broom is held! How gracefully the couple moves! As an ecstatic expression plays on the upturned face, a stunning pirouette is executed. At last, the dance is done. Receiving a fragrant bouquet of imagined red roses, the child bows repeatedly to an applause that no one else can hear.

A child will practice many styles as progress is made toward the preferred method of the adult sweeper. It should be an enjoyable pursuit. In truth, I would not sweep another floor if I found no pleasure in it. Nor should you. Likewise, neither should a child.

SEPTEMBER MOON WALK _____

THE MOON IS still more than half full... so bright that shadows separate on the wet grass around my mobile home on the road without a mailbox near the river without a name. The deck is dappled... wet and dry, dark and light. The knots peer up at me like suspicious eyes.

Sally and Sam, my miniature dachshunds, lead me along the gravel driveway. My blanket-swathed shadow looks like an old one leaning down, whispering to the earth... my tousled hair, like a grand feather-bonnet.

Acorns are falling around us. The garden shed stands elegantly, draped in mystery, its broken door askew. A gathering of nasturtium at the front... an army of sunflowers on the left. Beyond... tall aspen silvered in the moonlight.

The Frances Memorial Moon Garden bench welcomes me to sit and contemplate the night magic, while Sally and Sam sniff about trying to discover an insect or a mouse. The white-edged hosta is perfectly at home beside the old stump I carried out of the woods in the Lake 13 area. A parade of small, round stones from friend Ann Mikkelsen march along one edge of the sunken garden. Her father, Gordon, collected them.

Melissa's old sandbox marks the north-east corner. It has hosted a gay collection of poppies, now going persistently to seed. A boardwalk, softened by creeping phlox and capped by a large pale rock, carries the eye to a mixed garden of wildflowers, astilbe, day-lilies, blue hosta, and journey stones.

A brick path leads up two railroad-tie steps. The garden embraces me here... on either side, tall leafy stalks of flowers stand guarded by more stones from my journeys.

In the midst of all is a gravel bed that tempts the violas to leave their boundaries and bloom among the pea rock, now adorned with glowing maple leaves.

Something has struck the tree above me. Startled, I look up and see nothing. But I think it was a flying squirrel, coming home to the hollow maple after a long night of foraging.

The glossy, wet leaves are dripping with heavy dew.

Walking out onto the tarred road, I find it lost in fog on the west while the east glows with coming dawn.

An owl hoots down by the river, repeating its night song again and again like an ancient proverb.

Returning to the yard, I watch the house emerge from the fog like a lost ship abandoned by its captain... so, standing on the deck, I guide it through a misty sea.

Several small bells ring softly as I open and close the sturdy screen door. When I sit in the wicker rocker, I watch the clock announce 6:07 a.m. It's my favorite time of the day and night.

The crystals in the east window are already gathering light and bending it in pretty ways, while the bottles filled with small red grave-agates look forward to another Saturday morning.

Three tomatoes hug the edge of the window-sill, hoping to enjoy a sunny day, while my Arizona cactus quickly collects another burst of moonshine.

A wooden platter displays a proud collection of journey stones from the Black Hills. A black journey-stone, with amethyst-like veins marking its broken heart-shaped form, mourns endlessly.

In the west window still shrouded with the mystery of a foggy night, the ceramic hummingbird sprawls its wings in perpetual flight. Beside it, a "string-of-pearls" plant cascades from a suspended terra-cotta pot.

More and more light creeps into the room, and I return to bed for a few more winks. Moon walking is a glorious way to spend the night!

A foggy night reminds me of the wonderful Fog Woman.

IT HAPPENED ONE DAY in the long ago that a certain man was out in the bay, fishing with his two slaves.

Suddenly a heavy fog fell around them and they lost sight of the shore. Indeed, they were unable to see each other. For one moment, the fog swirled enough to allow the man to see... that a woman was sitting beside him.

She reached up, took the man's fine spruce-root hat from his head, and held it out in her right hand. The man was amazed to see all the fog rush into the hat. Now they could see the land, and the slaves quickly paddled the canoe to shore.

When the man saw that this woman had power over fog, he named her Fog Woman and took her for his wife.

The next day, he took one of his slaves out fishing with him. The older slave was left behind to watch the woman.

While Fog Woman waited for the men to return, she became quite hungry and told the slave to fill his hat with water and bring it to her. He did as he was told.

Then the woman dipped one finger into the water and told the slave to spill the water out on the ground. The slave thought it was foolishness, but he did as he was told.

Imagine his surprise when a great salmon came up

out of the wet ground and began flopping about.

Fog Woman told him to kill the fish quickly so it wouldn't suffer. Then she cleaned and cooked it.

Being satisfied, the slave and Fog Woman fell asleep. When the man returned, he noticed how happy his slave looked and how pleased Fog Woman appeared. He wanted to know if they would like to share the two bullheads he'd caught.

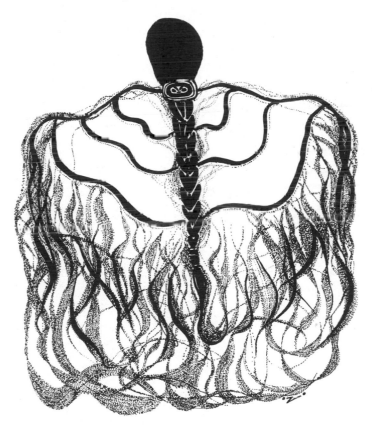

"No," Fog Woman said, "we've already eaten."

So the younger slave prepared the two little fish and the man ate them both, because they were too small to share.

One day, the old slave told the man about Fog Woman's power.

"She calls the salmon out of the ground," he said.

The man asked Fog Woman to show him this power and she did. He was thrilled.

"Now I will have much fish and I will never have to go fishing again. Make many salmon for me!" he ordered.

"No," the woman replied. "That would be wasteful. If you want many salmon, you must build a big smoke-house. When I see the smoke-house, I will know how many fish to call."

So the man and his slaves began working at once. Soon a great smoke-house stood beside the bay.

The man filled his hat with water and Fog Woman washed her hair in it. When he spilled the water out, the salmon came out of the ground in great abundance.

Quickly they were killed, cleaned, and hung in the smoke-house.

Now the man was satisfied, for he had much food.

For awhile he was happy with Fog Woman, but eventually he began to find fault with her. He complained frequently about the way she looked, the way she talked, the way she dressed. Even her laugh annoyed him.

One day Fog Woman told the man, "I've decided to return to my father's house."

The man was angry. "You're my wife!" he shouted. "You can't leave me."

"But," Fog Woman reasoned, "we are not happy. You seem to hate everything about me. I think you married me because of my power over the fog, and you want to keep me to call the salmon when the fish are gone."

When she stood to leave, the man became furious and struck her.

Immediately he apologized. "I'm sorry. You made me so angry that I forgot myself. Please forgive me. I'll never strike you again."

Fog Woman stared at him for several minutes. Then she said, "No, you're not sorry now. But you will be. I will forgive you, but I won't stay... and you will never strike me again."

To his surprise, Fog Woman untied her braid and combed her hair. Then she walked toward the bay.

The man shouted at her but she did not seem to hear. He ran after her and grabbed her. But she slipped out of his hands. He stood in her path but she passed through him like a spirit.

Suddenly a mighty wind rolled up from the bay and knocked down the smoke-house.

The man watched in helpless amazement as the salmon began following Fog Woman to the water.

They were dead and dried on land but when they

reached the water they were completely restored and living again.

When the salmon had all returned, Fog Woman stepped onto the water, walked far out into the bay, and disappeared in a heavy fog.

Many times the man thought of her... especially when he was hungry.

So the words of Fog Woman came true. For truly this was a sorry man... and, truly, he never hit that woman again.

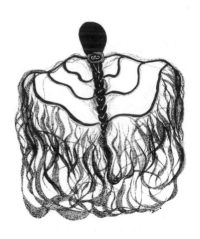

BUFFALO WIFE _____

WHEN THE LAND was full of buffalo, the people hunted them for food, clothing, tools, and shelter. However, the people were careful to take no more than was needed and had respect for the life of the buffalo that died... for in their death, the people lived.

But it happened that people grew careless and forgot to teach their children how important it was to honor the buffalo nation. So there grew up a generation who did not respect the buffalo. They hunted beyond their need and often allowed portions of the buffalo to be wasted.

Therefore, the buffalo nation called a council and it was decided that buffalo would no longer give up their lives for the people. They would not allow themselves to be killed.

It wasn't long before the people grew hungry and ragged. All manner of prayers were offered to Great Spirit concerning the pitiful condition of the people, but still they were not allowed to take a buffalo life.

One day, a young woman went to get water and saw a herd of buffalo standing on a high rocky ridge. She called to them, "Oh, buffalo brothers and sisters, we are hungry! Soon winter will be upon us and we will starve. Only with your help can we hope to go on living."

She was so concerned for the welfare of her people that she shouted, "If some of you will fall down and die,

I will marry a buffalo."

To her surprise, several buffalo stepped over the rocky ridge and plunged to their deaths. She ran to the village and told the other women what had happened. They followed her to the place where the dead buffalo lay.

How excited they were as they skinned the buffalo and prepared to carry the meat home! But suddenly, a very large buffalo bull came among them and told the young woman that he was her husband. He said she must go away with him according to her promise.

Without a word, she turned from her people and followed her husband.

Her family grieved for her all winter and in the spring, her father went out to find her. He searched all along the waterways and lakes, looking for her tracks. But it seemed hopeless.

"Perhaps," he thought sadly, "perhaps she has not survived."

But one day, he discovered the tracks of a young woman mingled with the tracks of many buffalo, and he knew that she was near. So he hid himself behind some rocks and waited to see if she would return.

Not far from there, the buffalo were grazing.

The buffalo husband said to his wife, "I'm thirsty and tired. I want you to go to the river and bring me some water."

So the young woman took her waterbag and went to the river. Her father saw her coming and ran to meet

her. What a happy reunion they had!

But after a short time the woman said, "I must return to my husband."

"No," her father said, "please return home with me."

The woman said, "I cannot. The welfare of all our people is in my hands."

When she left, her father hid behind the rocks again. He thought, "When she returns, I'll tell her how much we need her. I'm sure she can be persuaded to come home with me."

When she returned to her husband and put the waterbag down for him to drink, the bull said, "I smell a man."

The woman said, "You smell me."

"I smell a man!" the furious bull bellowed. "What kind of a woman are you! You went to the river to meet a man!"

"I went to the river to get water for you," she reminded him.

But he pawed the earth with his great black hooves and tossed his head in anger. "That man will die!" he roared.

Then he gathered other buffalo and they went to the river to kill the man. There, they trampled over his remains until there was nothing left of him.

When the woman arrived at the wallow, she fell down weeping in the place where her father's blood stained the earth.

"Who was this man?" the buffalo husband wanted

to know.

"He was my father," she replied.

The buffalo was surprised but he was still angry. "Do you grieve when the buffalo are killed?"

The young woman said, "My people perish, too."

Now the buffalo began to pity the woman and her people. "I'm sorry," he said at last. "Here's what we will do. If you can bring your father back to life, the buffalo will allow themselves to be killed by your people. But when you kill a buffalo you must honor that buffalo with a dance. If you do this, the spirit of the buffalo that died will be reborn in a buffalo calf and so... there will always be buffalo."

So, the woman asked a magpie bird to help her find a piece of her father's body that had not been broken by the buffalo. At last the magpie found a vertebrae bone and laid it in the woman's hand.

The woman carried it to the top of a high grassy hill and covered it with her robe. She sang and prayed for three days and when she raised the robe... there was her father's body, completely restored. But he was still dead.

So she covered the body and began to sing and pray again. In a few minutes, she raised the robe and her father opened his eyes.

Then he stood up and they walked back to where the bull was waiting.

When the buffalo saw the power that his wife had, he released her from the marriage.

The bull showed them how to dance. Then, he danced away to rejoin the herd.

The man and his daughter returned to the village and told the people what had happened and showed them the buffalo honoring dance.

As a result of this young woman's efforts to protect the welfare of her people, all nations still benefit from the life of the buffalo. Because many people continue to do this dance, there are still many buffalo today.

IT HAPPENED in the long ago that three women loved the same man. But the young man had determined that he would only choose one who was so kind and generous that her eyes were open to mysteries not seen by the selfish and the cruel.

His sister was such a woman, so he asked her to help him test the three women who loved him.

Now, the first two women were so ambitious to become the wives of this good man that they lied to his sister. They told her they saw things that no one else could see and described strange sights. Of course, the sister of the man knew the women were lying and reported this to her brother.

When the third woman was tested, she did not speak of the things which she saw. But she looked about her as though she took great joy in the ordinary things that we all see every day.

The sister of the young man recognized that this woman could see beyond the physical realm. "What do you see that gives you such pleasure?" she asked.

The young woman smiled. "I see what you see," she said.

Then the sister of the man knew that this woman would not lie to her. They sat together all that day discussing the wonderful things they saw. They became friends and a special love grew between them for they were of one spirit.

So the young man lived happily with his kind and generous wife. But the women who lied turned into trees.

The Mandan say they were the first aspen trees.

Now, the aspen grow in many places on Turtle Island, and just like the two jealous women... they gossip all the time.

IT HAPPENED in the long ago that Creator was watching some children at play near the center of a village in the west of Turtle Island. The children were laughing and singing.

But as she watched them, Creator became sad. "These children will grow old," she thought. "Their skin will wrinkle, their joints will ache, their teeth will fall out, some will go blind. The young hunters' strength will fail. The young women will lose their graceful step."

She looked at the playful puppies yapping happily around the children. "These too will grow old," Creator thought. "The fragrant and beautiful flowers will fade. The leaves of the trees will fall."

So Creator began to pity the things that had been made.

Now, it was in the fall of the year. It was still warm and the sun was shining. But Creator knew that winter was coming and with it... cold and hardship. Already the wind was carrying yellow leaves to the ground and swirling them about the children's feet.

Creator saw the sun casting shadows of dancing children upon the earth... she saw the bright colors of the flowers... she saw the gold of autumn leaves... she saw the blue of the sky....

Suddenly Creator smiled. "I will make something new. I will make something that will gladden my own heart. I will make something that will delight the children. I will make something that the old ones will also enjoy."

So Creator took a spot of golden sunshine, a handful of the blue sky, the green of pine, the white of corn, the black of infants' hair, the shades of changing leaves, the beauty of flowers, the glory of sunrise....

To all this, she added a song.

She put the new creations in a bag and took it to the children. "Children," Creator said, "this is for you."

She opened the bag and hundreds of colorful butterflies flew out. They fluttered around the children and settled on their hair. Then the butterflies left the children to sip the nectar of nearby flowers. Later, they gathered in the pine trees to sing.

Truly the children were amazed. They had never seen such a wonder. The Creator was satisfied.

But the birds were not pleased. For they had been allowed to sing only after a great competition. They had won their songs by flying as high as they could. Therefore, they felt it was not fair for Creator to give songs to the butterflies.

Creator considered the birds' complaint and agreed. It was not fair to give the butterflies a song, when the birds had needed to compete for theirs.

So Creator took the songs from the butterflies and that is why they are silent today. Still, they are beautiful... and still they gladden Creator's heart... and still they are the delight of children... and still the old ones enjoy them, too.

ONE PLACE TO TURN

MY JOB HAD BEEN finished for three weeks. The child-support check had been spent on bills and a car repair. Our wood heater was being fed one stick at a time to save wood, but we now had only three pieces left. My last twenty dollars would have to buy wood instead of food.

I looked at my children sitting around the table and asked Steven to bless the food before us. As we ate, I heard their young voices chattering about the events of the day, but I was not really listening. My thoughts were already on tomorrow. I wondered how many days would pass before I could assure my children there would be enough food for each tomorrow as it came.

My thoughts were interrupted for a moment when Esther asked me to make cookies. I told her we had no sugar and no flour. She skipped out of sight without seeming too disappointed.

Knowing that at least we would have firewood, I encouraged myself by remembering that the worst of the winter was over. Then, Great Spirit began to remind me of past blessings.

I had prayed for a winter coat. My old one had become so worn it was no longer warm enough for another Minnesota winter. In a short time, a woman brought me a good coat. The next day, a lady gave me a second good coat, and on a later day, I received a third.

My children needed a bed. Soon after, a man called and asked if we could use a bed. He said it had been given to him but he didn't need it. He even delivered it right to our door.

Thanksgiving came. "How will I tell the children we will have no turkey this year?" I had wondered. As I entered the house, the children greeted me with loud excitement. They said a man had been there and left a big turkey for us.

Annette wanted to play the piano, but there was no way we could buy one. I sent my prayers skyward. In a couple of weeks, a family moving to Puerto Rico asked if we would accept their piano as a gift to the children. Of course we accepted.

My son had received a graft in his ear. One day he began to cry out in pain and blood began to flow from that ear. I hurried him to the doctor. He said the graft had ruptured... they would need to repeat the surgery. There was little I could do, but my son asked, "Mother, could we pray together?" The doctor examined him again two weeks later. The ear was healed and the doctor could not even find the scar.

My little daughter fell sick. The doctor found blood in her urine. He scheduled a scan, planning to inject dye into her kidneys and take x-rays. I asked Great Spirit for help. On the day of the scan, her urine was tested again. The doctor found no blood. The scan was cancelled.

I had been advised to accept the fact that my infant son would not be normal. He would not ever walk, or talk, or feed himself, the doctor said. I prayed. It was a very surprised doctor who later told me that the disease of congenital hydrocephalus had been arrested without treatment. The boy grew up to walk and talk and help himself.

One evening, I was at a community sing when it began to storm. I was worried because my roof leaked in several places. My biggest concern was that the boys' bed would be too wet to sleep in. I prayed about it. When we got home, I checked the bed right away and found it dry. That part of the roof has not leaked since!

As I thought of these things, my spirit was built up. At noon the next day, two friends arrived with food for us. In the bags, we found the cookies Esther had asked for. No wonder she had not been disappointed! In another bag, I found the sugar and flour I needed.

Filled with thankfulness, I wondered, "Is anything too hard for faith to overcome?" As I looked at the groceries on the table in front of me, I knew the answer would always be "no."

Still... I often wondered about that roof. I couldn't understand how it would just stop leaking, but I never spoke to anyone about it.

After many years, my dad told me he'd noticed the stain on the ceiling when he'd come to visit me. He'd gone home to Minneapolis, but it bothered him so much that he'd returned with tools and tar to fix my roof.

When he got to Cass Lake, no one was home. He found our ladder, climbed up on the roof, and began to work. He took his time, but still no one came. So he drove back to Minneapolis without telling anyone what he'd done.

Knowing this does not diminish my confidence in the power of faith... it sweetens my father's memory.

BLUEBERRY JOY

WHEN THE CHILDREN were very young I took them berry picking. At first they would help me pick the small but flavorful fruit with great enthusiasm, but by and by, they tired of a task grown tedious. I gave them each a small container and when they had filled it, they could resign from berry picking for the day.

I tied a white cloth up in a tree and told them not to go so far that they couldn't see it. I picked nearby, and then when the berries were depleted, I'd move the children and the cloth to an unpicked area.

I usually had a baby to breastfeed or diaper, so I returned to check on the children at frequent intervals. I usually found them busy with games or amusing the baby. They didn't seem to mind being in the woods. We lunched on sandwiches and tea.

They knew I would not leave until I'd filled my five-gallon pail. So they did not complain.

When the pail was full, I tied a dishtowel over the top to avoid spilling any fruit. I packed up the remaining food and tied small bundles for the children to carry. Then I tied the blanket into a baby-sling. Picking up the pail and the bundles, we were ready to leave.

They followed me cheerfully out of the woods. We packed everything into our old station wagon and bumped happily along the two-rut roads back to the tarred highway.

These were long and tiring days, but we did this as often as possible so we'd have plenty of berries during the winter.

Many times during the cold days that followed, I'd open a jar of fragrant blueberries and remind the children of how they'd helped to pick them. I think they enjoyed them more for having shared in the challenge of the harvest.

When I recall those pleasant days... I can almost hear the flies buzzing around my face, feel the hot sun on my head, and in the distance... I catch the sound of children laughing in the fields of blueberry joy.

WINTER

WINTER

THE PERFECT GIFT

THE FROZEN GROUND sounded hollow under Willy's heavy boots. After every few steps, he would turn to look back toward the sleeping village. The little cluster of houses seemed so far away. He knew that soon he would not be able to see them at all.

Willy had gotten up early and dressed quietly. Then he'd made two peanut butter sandwiches, filled his battered thermos with last night's tea, put the lunch in his backpack, closed the door softly and set off for the far end of the island.

Grandmother was ill and Willy knew this would be their last winter together. For a long time, he had tried to think of a last gift he could bring to her. It would have to be a very special gift. Finally, he'd decided and made his careful plan.

The heavy, gray sky stretched over the land. Looking back, he could no longer see the village. For one awful moment he felt like running back to the safety and warmth of Grandmother's old house.

Instead, he took a deep breath, looked at his pocket compass, and set off toward the distant coast with a more determined step.

A sudden wind hit Willy like a spray of ice water. He shivered and pulled his furry parka hood close around his face. Peering into the heavy fog, he felt as if he were being swallowed up by a hungry white monster. His heart began to beat painfully in his chest. Then he remembered the talk he'd had with Grandmother last night.

He could almost see her, almost hear her speaking. "Willy," she had said, "when I'm afraid, I remind myself that I can always trust Great Spirit to help me."

Suddenly Willy felt very safe. "Yes," he told himself, "it's foolish to be frightened. Great Spirit is here with me."

At last he reached the coast. He looked out at the green-gray sea. The water came rolling up over the rocky shore. Then he sat down to eat his lunch.

Willy sat for a long time, watching the sea as it reached up to grasp the land only to fall back again and gather itself up for another rush up the rocks.

Then he began walking up the shore looking for the cobblestone cove. After a few minutes, he reached that particular place where the water tumbled the rocks in a manner that made the beach appear paved with round stones. Then he began to search for the most beautiful rock.

Finally Willy selected a round, black stone and wrapped it in his scarf. He placed it in his pack and turned back toward home.

Two hours later, Grandmother saw him returning. She saw how he held his shoulders square as he picked his way confidently across the familiar frozen landscape. She could tell it had been a good day for Willy.

While Willy warmed himself near the woodburning cookstove, Grandmother pressed fresh bread dough into small biscuits. Later, they dipped the warm bread into steaming bowls of bean soup and sipped cups of honey-sweetened tea. Grandmother was beginning her second cup when Willy pushed himself away from the table.

Quietly he lifted his backpack from its peg on the wall and carried it to the table. Reaching into the pack, he pulled out his bulging scarf and placed it on the table in front of Grandmother.

Slowly she opened the bundle and picked up the

stone. She closed her fingers around it and held it tight.

Willy watched with pride and quiet excitement. The stone looked so smooth and shiny, so warm and heavy in Grandmother's thin, wrinkled hand.

Grandmother smiled at the gift for a long time. Then she smiled at Willy. Her tired eyes were bright with happiness.

"Yes," Willy thought, "it is a perfect gift."

THE SONG OF THE FLUTE _____

WHEN THE FAMILY and friends of Lizzy Mason gathered around her large and bountiful table at her Redby home on Easter Sunday, 1979, they did not know that the song had begun.

Annie was a child then, and so was relegated neither to the head of the table nor to the end. She took her seat at right center and, bowing her young head, listened to Mother's Easter prayer.

Her childish dreams were not forgotten as Mother asked a personal blessing on each one present. Annie was thankful that Mother was not long-winded and soon, a thick slab of succulent ham was laid on her plate.

The meal was crowned with a wedge of blueberry pie for all... berries Lizzy had picked while being assaulted by deer flies and mosquitoes. So it was relished all the more.

Soon after the feast, the center leaf of the table was removed and placed in the shed for storage Eventually the old walnut table was gifted to a nephew in Minneapolis. The leaf, it seemed, had been forgotten.

Many snows would fall on the old shed roof and many a spider would weave in the rafters before the forgotten leaf would find itself at the center of things again.

In the spring of 1989, Ruggie Mason, the flute master, needed a piece of good wood. Several pieces had been scrutinized and set aside when the walnut leaf was discovered in the shed. Ten years of dust was wiped away by the craftsman's hand, the expert eye gave its appraisal, and soon the wood was approved.

The flute master knows that each flute has its own song. This is his work. Though he himself cannot play the flute, he alone can give the flute its song.

The flute was barely begun when it was laid aside, while the sugar bush was worked. When the flute master returned, he took up other tasks. A pipe stem was made, a stone bowl carved, a bear-claw necklace completed.

Many flutes had been begun, and some were ruined in haste. Six of them lay rotting in the woods behind the shed. This is work for unhurried hands.

At last, he was ready. He laid his careful hand upon the flute. Many times he turned it as the holes were precisely executed. Many times he placed it to his lips and listened with his heart as the flute searched for its song.

Then he did not pick it up for many days, as he raised the diamonds on a willow walking stick. But he thought about it always and as he did, he began to hear the song it was trying to sing.

At last, at last... it was done. It was beautiful to see. It was wonderful to touch. It was ready to sing. So he tied the moose-hide thong over the birchbark reed and wrapped the flute in a soft cloth.

From the day he'd discovered the dusty table-leaf, the flute master had known who would play the song that the flute carried in its heart.

Now, as there is a time for everything under the sun, it would soon be time to gift the flute. So it was carried to Cass Lake and presented to Annie at the home of her maternal grandmother, *Waseygabowikwe*.

The flute was unwrapped, passed to her over a formica table-top, and laid in both her hands. It was graciously accepted. "*Mii-gwetch*," she said softly, her eyes bright with unspoken pleasure.

She lifted the flute to her lips, listened to its tone, and played its perfect scale. The flute master smiled, nodding his head slowly. He was satisfied.

The flute was taken home and there, beside the river, it began to teach Annie its song. Sometimes she could not play at all. Her hand was not unhurried. Her soul wanted tenderness. Her heart was deaf

But the day came when the song of the flute flowed sweet and certain. Then it was carried to White Earth in a deer-skin bag.

There, as the body of a loved one was lowered into earth's embrace, the flute raised its voice. The wind carried the song to each listener, drawing mournful hearts together like shining beads on a glass thread.

Now, each has gone on their way... but the song of the flute goes on, too. Perhaps someday you will hear it... carried on a wind that danced that day on the far-off hill... *Ahnwebiyan*, Place of Rest.

THE NUTHATCHES and the chickadees are busy at the feeder. The chickadees break out in frequent song, declaring their joy on this bright fall morning.

I saw a robin, too. I thought they had all flown south. John said he saw a robin yesterday, probably the same one... a bird too old for another long flight, perhaps deciding this is a good place to die.

Here in the yard swing, I can survey my flower gardens... once so bright with vivid blooms. Now even the yellow mums have turned to tarnished gold. I can smell the fallen leaves, dried and crusty underfoot, their fragrance so brave... so sad.

It has been another bad year for our birch trees. The old ones are dead, the younger ones struggle. But the new birch, just a bit taller than me, seem full of energy and promise.

The windbreak of evergreen that John and I planted along the north road stands like a small parade of soldiers just learning to march. Some are too tall, some too short... there is no order in their ranks. Still, they do look full of honor and I will see them grown, mature and beautiful someday.

If you had seen this place when we came to live here! So wild, and brushy, and inhospitable. But we have made a home and gardens and a place where people come to rest... and one by one they say, "It is a place of peace."

Last year the blue-jay population was in demise. This year we have so many. I hope I can feed all our winter birds. The jays can be so aggressive and unkind... but they also must eat.

Sparrows and juncos are ground-feeding all around me. Yesterday I took an injured junco home and made her a nest and kept her warm. She laid for over an hour without moving. At last, she hopped out of her bed and flew up to perch on my string-of-pearls plant. She watched her fellow juncos outside, then she fluttered against the window. She kicked my large old blue-glass Vick's bottle off the window edge. It shattered on the floor, and my grave-agates tumbled across the carpet. I caught the junco and carried her outside, but it was too cold and my hand was too comfortable to abandon.

So back in the house we went. I put her down and she hopped across the carpet. I think she was looking for food. After another hour, I carried her out and put her on the top rail of the deck. I sat nearby and guarded her from our curious dogs. Immediately she went to sleep! But at last her eyes popped open, she shook her wings, and flew away.

A thin gray cloud-cover has veiled the sun and brought a chill over the day. I should feel cheated out of my sun-day, but I do not. John is piling brush for winter fires in the woods. He has one burning now and the smoke feels sharp in my nose. Oh, if only you could see the fire dancing at night! It's so terribly beautiful that it almost breaks my heart.

The white oaks stand leafless... their twisted branches dark against the sky. The little red oaks wear their leaves with quiet dignity, for they alone know one of the Great Spirit's most important mysteries. The red pine behind the dog kennel looks a bit droopy... I shall have to encourage it to grow straight and tall. John and I planted it, an eight-inch seedling, no more than six years ago.

The lodgepole pine is dead and rusty. But John will not pull it up. "Give it a chance," he says.

The three junipers are new. We planted them in September. If they survive the winter, they should do well.

My little rose-bush, the single survivor of six, has four unopened buds... pink, pretty, frozen. The johnny jump-ups have pushed their purple faces through the leafy mulch to watch the snow coming to cover them up.

Cheyenne and I planted a blue spruce last fall. It looks good, small but healthy.

I crushed a wild mint between my fingers and of course, it offered all its captive sunshine and summer showers in an unforgettable aroma. Oh, is there anything like it?

There are three large tamaracks on this land. They are bronze now and dropping their needles. What a story they tell to those familiar with Ojibwe lore.

At the end of the woods is a great elm, with seven

huge limbs growing out of its massive trunk. It died last winter. It's the prettiest of all our leafless trees now. It would make a perfect place for a tree house. If I were a child, I'd build a house there.

The little river is flowing. Soon ice will lace its edges and eventually, winter will lock it in. The sad remains of the wonderful beaver dam reflects itself in the dark water.

It was a much younger John who planted spruce near his parents' house. At least a dozen have survived.

Behind the old house a white oak was cut down, and from the stump so many branches grow that it looks like a friendly forest Medusa.

Amidst the rubble, an old rice boat is rotting. A bundle of cedar floats are being nibbled away by moss and mice and lichens.

The beaver are still coming to the point to cut food. They are not far away and I am glad. I hope the trappers don't come to this place of peace to kill these beavers. Oh, he is such a noble little brother.

I could not resist gathering poplar tops for the beaver. I spent about an hour climbing over logs left by the little choppers. I also built a small observation platform. When the moon is full, I'll come out and watch the beaver work.

John and I are making a trail on the south side of this land. I hope one day to put in new trees. I want to restore the red cedar and white pine that must have grown here before the loggers came. Of course, the great piliated woodpecker that lives in these woods loves the old standing dead trees. But they are falling all the time. With every storm a few more come crashing down.

I can climb up into the arms of a giant poplar full of years. It fell long ago but it is still propped up on strong limbs. Cheyenne and I used to picnic here. She hasn't been here since last year. She's seven now... perhaps I should seek a younger tree-picnic companion. The trunk is crusted with white fungus, like sea shells adorning an old ship.

Oh, such a splendid adventure this has been... and I did not even cross the road.

A FTER TWO DAYS of wind and storm, I have gone out to discover the magic of new snow.

It's here in my summer camp! Magic!

The fireplace, once sizzling hot, is piled with snow. My old work-gloves, still pinned to the clothes line, are pointing empty fingers toward the town of Walker. I left the gloves there for a spider which had made herself comfortable in one soiled palm. I left both gloves because I could not see the use of wearing one.

The woodpile is waiting patiently for next year's summer camp. The empty, unreplenished bird-feeder pivots on the wind.

There is no place the wind has not been, sculpting the landscape to perfection. Even now, eagerly licking at something left undone... it finishes the picture for me.

The rusty old cot welcomes me and I sit down. But it offers less comfort now, and I find it difficult to imagine that I actually slept here, warm and cozy, not many weeks ago.

A ribbon of mouse-tracks leads me to a tiny hole where Ms. Mouse searched for food and shelter. I can almost see her scurry through the darkness... her small ears folded down to keep warm, her eyes alert for an overhead attack.

Following a rabbit trail, I find a fallen oak. Underneath I see the tramped-down place where a rabbit waited nervously before hurrying on.

Everywhere the squirrels have been digging up their stored food.

My brush-pile shelters are being put to use as winter habitat. Two large green fallen poplars will provide wood for many fires. I see rabbits have been nibbling away the tender twig-bark.

No beaver activity here... perhaps they are ice-locked.

I T HAPPENED in the long ago that an old man lived alone in the great pine forest.

One day, three fierce warriors that had been banished from another village because of their very poor conduct discovered the old man. And because he was old, and because he was alone, they decided to take everything from him that was of any value to them.

They took his robes and hides. They took his tools and hunting bows. They took his arrows and knife. They took his food and clothes. They took his moccasins and mittens. Then they burned down his lodge.

They were about to take his life, when the old man shouted. "Stop! You cannot kill me, for it is not my time to die."

The fierce warriors were surprised at the boldness of this brief speech. While they hesitated, the old man continued to speak.

"See those trees?" he said, pointing toward the east. "The Great Spirit gave those trees to me. He told me that I would not die until the leaves of those trees failed to remain on their branches through the long winter."

Now the three warriors had never seen this particular tree before, but they knew that all trees lost their leaves in the fall and stood leafless during the winter.

So one of the men said, "Very well, old man, we will not kill you today. But we will return when snow covers the land. Then we will see. If the trees have no leaves, you will die. I myself will kill you. That is my promise."

"I will be here," the old man replied. "I'm not going away. This is my home. I will be waiting here for you. My word is good."

So the three men went away and the old man began to rebuild his lodge and restore his food supply.

When the land was covered with snow, the three fierce warriors returned to kill the old man. But when they saw that the trees which the old man had received from the Great Spirit were still covered with dry leaves, they knew they could not take his life. So they went away without bothering him.

But each winter, they returned to see if it was time for the old man to die. They discovered something strange about this man. For while they grew older and older... he remained unchanged.

Eventually, the three warriors died.

The elders say that from this place near the old man's lodge, the red oak has scattered itself across the land. They say, perhaps, the old man still lives today.

They also say that many things have changed. They say the Ojibwe are losing their values. That we have retained certain empty customs, but the traditions which kept the Ojibwe strong are being lost. They say that when the red-oak leaves fail to remain on the trees through the winter... there will be no more Anishinabe Ojibwe. A culture will be gone forever.

IT WOULD BE an exciting Christmas program! We'd practiced for weeks.

My role was simple... stand and sing, with about twenty other eager first-grade children.

We gathered at St. Stephen's Catholic School in Minneapolis, about four blocks from my grandparents' home on Franklin Avenue. Grandma wore a navy blue dress sprinkled with tiny white flowers, her Sunday hat, and a dress-up coat.

She'd be so proud, I promised myself. I really felt quite important. I would give her such a gift! We would enjoy it together forever.

But Grandma had poor eyesight, and just before I was marched backstage she whispered, "Stand where I can see you."

From the stage, I looked out at a sea of largely unknown faces. Grandma was in the third row. She glanced about anxiously. "She can't see me," I thought.

Quickly I stepped out of line and stood between the rows of singing children.

Then Grandma nodded and smiled up at me.

Afterwards the teacher took me aside. "You ruined the program," she scolded. "Everyone else stood in their proper row. But you spoiled it by standing between the rows!"

Soon Grandma came. She helped me into my coat,

cap, and mittens. Then she took my hand and we walked home.

"You looked so nice," she said. "It was a good program. You did your very best and I'm proud of you."

The teacher may have been disappointed but Grandma was quite pleased. Therefore, I was elated.

When I recall that night, I can't help but smile at the skinny, knock-kneed girl with the long braids and the big teeth. That's her... standing between the rows.

I see Grandma, too. There she is in the third row, smiling up at me.

TAMARACK AND CHICKADEE _____

IT HAPPENED in the long ago that Tamarack was ever-green, like the red pine. The Ojibwe say its beautiful, green, cone-shaped form graced the woodlands all through the long winter.

One day during a terrible storm, Chickadee was injured. He was nearly dead from cold. The little bird struggled through the blowing snow until he stood at the foot of the tall Tamarack.

"Please drop some of your lower branches to shelter me from the storm," Chickadee cried. "Oh, that I might live!"

"I should say not," Tamarack quickly replied. "I did not grow beautiful green branches to break them off for you. I'm sorry, but I prefer to keep my fine form."

So Chickadee pulled his small battered body to the root of the tall Red Pine.

"Please drop some of your lower branches to shelter me from the storm," Chickadee cried. "Oh, that I might live!"

Red Pine pitied Chickadee and quickly dropped enough branches to shelter the little bird.

Now, Great Spirit saw what had happened and said to Red Pine, "From this day you will always drop your lower branches to remind others that you paid a high price so a small bird could live."

When Tamarack heard this, he was glad he had not

dropped any of his branches.

"Now," he thought, "I will keep my fine form."

"Yes, Tamarack," Great Spirit said, "you will keep your fine form. But from this day, your needles will begin to turn brown, then they will fall off. Soon you will die and be forgotten."

Tamarack wept. "The punishment is too harsh," he cried.

Chickadee had crept out from under the red-pine branches lying on the snow. He pitied Tamarack.

"Oh, Great Spirit," Chickadee prayed. "Please don't let Tamarack die and be forgotten."

"Very well," Great Spirit said to Chickadee.

Then turning to Tamarack, Great Spirit added, "You will not die and be forgotten. But every autumn, your fine green needles will turn brown and fall off. Then you will stand naked in the forest all winter, as a reminder to others that it is always better to be kind and merciful than it is to be vain and selfish."

MOON DAUGHTER _____

IT HAPPENED one day, not so very long ago, that a precious Moon Daughter slipped quietly away from her sky home and came to dwell on earth.

She heard the rumble of distant wars and saw the dead of many nations.

She learned that war-makers were rich powerful men who never died in bloody fields. Indeed, it was the young and poorly educated who were called to protect the artificial boundaries established by long-gone kings, and re-established by proud rulers of each new age.

She read of marvelous weapons, so effective that whole cities could be destroyed in seconds. Entire populations... gone.

She attended universities and pondered how it was that so many of these educated people seemed to remain ignorant.

When she turned to the elders, she found that great numbers of them had grown sick and foolish.

At last, the lonely Moon Daughter realized the futility of remaining on earth. She decided to return to her home in the sky.

One night under a full winter moon, she waited for the old instructions to come to her... but they did not.

Fearfully she stared at the moon and willed it to speak... but it was silent.

Frantically she built a fire and, cutting off her hair,

threw it into the leaping flames. The acrid smoke rose high... but the moon no longer recognized the odor of her daughter's hair.

Now Moon Daughter knew the dreaded truth! She could never return... for she'd been gone too long. She'd learned too much of earthly things and had forgotten the ancient wisdoms of the moon.

Eventually she lost herself in a large city and joined the homeless throngs. There she remains to this day... chanting moon maxims while pushing her wobbly-wheeled grocery cart down noisy, filthy streets.

That's her... in the green hat with the red-silk rose corsage tucked into the third buttonhole of her baggy blue sweater.

Wait! Moon Daughter! Wait! I, too, have heard the magic. Together we can remember the ancient instructions.

But full of fear, she abandons the cart and runs from me. I follow... but soon I'm too breathless to continue.

Returning to the abandoned cart, I see the rose corsage laying on the cold concrete. With careful fingers I pick it up, place it gently in my pocket, and carry it home.

I still have that faded rose corsage. If you don't believe me... ask the moon.

THE COIN _____

I T WAS THE WINTER of 1945 and twelve-year-old Billy Whitefeather had been working for Mary Kingbird all week. Yesterday she had promised, "When you finish the job, I'll pay you for the work you've done."

Now, Billy flogged himself with his long arms and stamped his feet as he waited for Mary to answer his knock. The December cold pressed through his worn jacket. He pulled his cap down closer around his ears. He cupped his hands over his mouth and blew some warmth into his ragged mittens. Then he folded his arms across his chest and tucked his hands under his arms. He turned to study the neatly stacked pile of split wood near the back of the house. "It will last for several weeks," he thought.

He remembered the sweat and toil... the heavy ax raised again and again... the long hours... walking home alone in the cold darkness. He felt he'd been measured and proven. Then the door opened, and Billy turned to find Mary looking out at him. "Are you finished already?" she asked.

Billy nodded. Mary leaned out and peered toward the woodpile. Then she slipped her twisted fingers into a small beaded purse hanging from her belt. The fingers wormed painfully in the bag, then emerged and pressed a coin into Billy's mitten. "*Mii-gwetch*," he said as he backed away from the door. He turned and quickly stepped off the sagging porch.

Billy did not look at the coin as he trudged along the trail from Mary's tired-looking house. He held it tightly while a lump thickened in his aching throat. "Oh," he moaned toward a watchful chickadee, "she only gave me a quarter." How terribly disappointed he was. "But," he consoled himself, "twenty-five cents added to the seventy-five cents I already have will still buy a good gift for Mother."

He hurried down the hill. When he was sure that Mary could no longer see him, he stopped to put the coin in his pocket. Tears filled his eyes as he stared in disbelief at the shiny nickel. He let the coin slide off his mitten and watched it roll down the trail a short distance. "She cheated me," Billy hissed between clenched teeth.

He wanted to return to Mary's house, to push over the woodpile and throw the wood out into the brush. But he also wanted to obey his mother. "Billy," she'd told him many times, "always show respect for your elders."

Late the next day, Mary arrived at Billy's house carrying a bundle under her arm.

Billy's mother quickly placed a chair near the wood

stove and the older woman sat down. Soon a cup of maple-sweetened swamp tea was brought to the visitor. After she had sipped at the hot tea for several minutes, Mary said, "I have something for Billy."

She handed the package to him. "Open it," she urged. Her soft voice was full of kindness and her dark eyes were full of pleasure. "You did a good job for me, but you worked too quickly," she told him. "You finished your work before I finished my work for you."

Carefully Billy laid the package on the table. Slowly he opened it. Inside was a pair of beaded deer-skin mittens.

"Put them on," coaxed Mary.

The smoky smell of newly-tanned hide filled the room. Billy pushed his hand into the soft rabbit-fur lining. The mink-trimmed cuffs reached halfway up to his elbow.

They were the finest mittens he'd ever seen. He stared at the intricate floral designs and thought of Mary's small, twisted fingers holding the fine beading needle. He thought of her old eyes finding the tiny beads. He thought of the woodpile still standing in neat stacks near her house.

"*Mii-gwetch*, Grandmother," he whispered.

Mary smiled.

When she was ready to leave, Billy put on his jacket, cap, and new mittens. "I'll walk with you," he said, offering her his strong arm.

Billy's mother watched them walk slowly down the

trail into the gathering darkness. Then she turned from the steamy window to set the table for supper. She thought of the shiny nickel she'd found on the trail that morning. She took the coin from her pocket and slid it under Billy's plate.

A GOOD NAME FOR BAD BOY

FATHER HAD SENT Bad Boy to the hated mound again. He spent many terrible hours there.

From the mound, he could see his mother's broad back, bent over the cooking pot. He knew she grieved for him.

Suddenly, his father stepped out of their lodge and stood for a long time looking toward the mound where Bad Boy was squatting. The boy imagined his father overcome by many evil things, and was frightened to find so much pleasure in it.

Bad Boy's mother watched her troubled son, sifting sand through his fingers, pretending not to notice the other boys playing nearby. She heard the younger children taunting and saw Bad Boy quiver with anger, but he did not leave the mound. So when a child poked Bad Boy with a long stick, she went out to the mound and sent the children away.

"The mound is not good," she thought. "My husband believes this will correct our son and teach him to be a good person... a strong person. But this is a great mistake."

On the following day, she prepared food and invited her husband to taste it. He complained that the soup was not good. She explained that it had been cooked in a bad kettle, and one should expect bad soup from such a kettle.

He picked up a piece of bread and put it back, saying, "It smells very bad."

Mother replied, "I cooked it with bad grease."

That night, Bad Boy's father crept among the sleeping forms on the lodge floor. He rolled Bad Boy out of his robe, put his big hand over the boy's mouth and with hand signals directed him outside.

Quickly Bad Boy was on his feet and left the lodge behind his father.

Bad Boy's mind was full of questions as they walked in silence through the quiet village and out into the surrounding darkness.

It was still dark when Mother opened her eyes. The first thing she saw was the empty robes. Smiling, she laid a few sticks of wood on the small fire, picked up her basket, and went to the mound.

Bad Boy and his father climbed to the top of a high hill. They sat together on the cold rocks. At last, Bad Boy saw his father stretch his hand toward the horizon. The sky had begun to announce the rising sun.

"Today, Bad Boy is dead," his father said. "Today, you are my son, Red Sky."

When they returned, the village was bustling with the usual early-morning activities, but Red Sky was seeing everything with new eyes.

He noticed that the mound was gone and could almost see his mother carrying it to the river... one basketful at a time.

Red Sky pulled back his shoulders as he walked.

"A good name must be carried with honor," he thought.

WHEN SANTA CAME TO VISIT_____

WHEN JOHN WAS a child he looked forward to Christmas with eager expectation, just as all children do.

On Christmas Eve, several Ojibwe families would gather at the central home and wait for Santa to arrive. Eventually they would hear the jingle of sleigh bells outside. Then, a knock at the door.

One of the men would go to see who the visitor might be. "Why, it's Santa," he'd announce in amazement. "He's really here!"

Santa would enter with a gunny-sack full of gifts. He'd give out the gifts. But no one would open them until everyone had received a package.

Afterwards Santa would sit with the families. They would drink tea and eat cookies. He'd talk with the men. He'd tell the children to be good. He'd thank the women for the Christmas treats.

Then he would leave. The families sat quietly and listened to the sleigh bells grow fainter and fainter.

"The best thing about Santa was that he spoke Ojibwe," John tells me. "I always felt proud about that. It meant that Santa Claus was an Indian... just like us."

FRANKLIN AVENUE CHRISTMAS _____

IT WAS GOING TO BE my fifth Christmas. But it would be my first Christmas in the city. I had gone to live with my maternal grandparents on Franklin Avenue in Minneapolis.

I sat in the front bay window watching the corner where Grandpa Vanoss would step out of the brightly-lit streetcar. My breath soon fogged the glass, and I began to draw a picture.

My finger traced the outline of a red barn, a small white house, and several sheds. I saw a nameless child walking through the snowy hills.

The tall barn was surrounded by white-bright snow... snow so clean, it looked like crystal beads sewn to a shining landscape, sparkling all around. I laid my finger against the glitter and it melted into a single drop that ran down the glass like a great lonely tear.

Suddenly Grandpa was beside me. "My girl," he said as he rubbed his cold nose against my cheek.

The farm fell away as I turned from the dirty mounds of Franklin Avenue snow and looked into Grandpa's kind eyes.

"What do you want for Christmas?" he asked from under his trim gray moustache.

"A farm," I whispered. "A big farm... with a horse, a dog, a cow, and sheep and chickens, too."

He smiled. "We'll let Santa know that you have

asked for a farm."

Then he stretched his tall thin body and went to sit in his rocking chair.

The next morning, he put on his heavy brown jacket, wrapped his black wool muffler around his neck, and pulled a furry cap over his shiny white hair. I ran to the door and caught his big hand in mine.

"Goodbye, Grandpa," I said, hoping he would ask me to go with him.

But he picked me up and set me down in the big chair by the bay window. Then he opened the door and went out into the dirty Franklin Avenue winter.

The next morning, I was awakened by Grandma. Shaking me gently, she whispered, "Wake up, my girl. Come and see what Santa has brought for you."

"A farm... is it a farm?" I wanted to know.

"Come and see," was all she said.

As I pulled on my socks, I could already see Grandma feeding our new chickens... Grandpa hitching our new horse to a blue sleigh. I heard a friendly puppy yapping at my heels as I ran to the front room.

Grandpa was sitting in his chair smoking his cigar. He was looking at me. I could see the happy sparkle in his old eyes as he said, "Santa has been here."

I looked under the tree and saw a small red barn surrounded by toy animals. I wanted to cry... but Grandpa was watching and he was so happy. I felt the tears sting in my eyes but caught them as they leaped forward. I swallowed the thick lump that had formed in my throat and sat down on the floor.

Slowly, I picked up the little black horse. My fingers felt his body grow warm as a faint heartbeat began tapping against my thumb. He grew a fine coat of sleek hair and wriggled out of my hand. I watched him gallop across the snowy fields toward the tall red barn... and laughed as the frightened chickens came to life in a flurry of white wings.

WINTER WALK

A FTER A HEAVY NIGHT MIST, every grass and twig wore winter gems. The forest nation awakened to another silver morning.

Brother Fox had left his dainty tracks on the snowy river, and I imagine muskrat, beaver, and otter eating at their leisure under the ice that keeps their secrets.

Lady is missing again. I haven't seen her for a week. I hope that she is well and enjoying the friendship of caring people somewhere. I pray she is not dead or suffering in a neglected trap.

Fox has hunted the meadow and I walk beside his stealthy steps. Looking back, it appears that we journeyed together across the wide field.

An old brush-pile under a tall spruce becomes a comfortable bench. Leaning against the great trunk, I recall another visit to this place.

It was several years ago when I watched a winter white weasel step silently into my range of vision, then disappear into the brush-pile. A moment later I felt watched... and looking about, discovered that I was being appraised by the glittering black eyes of the curious little hunter.

Suddenly he ducked out of sight to reappear about three feet from me. He stared at me intently for several more seconds, then popped back into the brush-pile. I didn't see him again....

Today, the shadows are richly blued as every little snowflake reflects tiny pieces of the December sky.

A clump of great white birch sheds another skin, and the ragged edges of torn bark wave gently in the slight breeze.

A bird calls from far away and is greeted by a relative closer to me. I hear their calls join in the distance, then disappear together.

Behind me, Squirrel is scolding someone... perhaps it is me. "Intruder! Intruder!" he cries.

Well, I am a bit chilly... so I move on.

Quite by accident, I have followed Fox home and discover his cozy earthen den.

Later, I approach a gathering of cedar trees and after picking a few aromatic twigs, I find I have stumbled upon a nicely secluded hideaway.

Tramping about a bit, I discover a great sprawling spruce. I can imagine this place in April or May. What a wonderful spring campsite this will be! I'll bring the grandchildren! The tent will look so snug under the huge tree. I'll wear my knee-high boots and explore the little wetland below the hill.

Even now, I'm tempted to enter the swamp and cross through to the road beyond, but I decide to follow my tracks back toward home.